Documents in Contemporary History

Britain and European integration since the Second World War

This lively new source book tells the story of Britain's hesitant moves into Europe, through a fascinating selection of recent documents from the Public Record Office and from diaries, memoirs and newspaper articles. The arguments on sovereignty and monetary union which helped destroy Thatcher and continue to threaten the stability of the Major government reach back in recognisable form to administrations presided over by Wilson, Callaghan, Macmillan and Eden and their responses to such problems is the central theme of this text.

Through its introductory sections, the book provides an assessment of the debates and controversies surrounding Britain's attitudes towards European integration and a valuable collection of source material for students of modern history and politics and for those who wish to have a wider understanding of Britain's place in the contemporary world.

Sean Greenwood is Head of the Department of History and Reader in Modern History at Canterbury Christ Church College.

Documents in Contemporary History is a series designed for sixth-formers and undergraduates in higher education: it aims to provide both an overview of specialist research on topics in post-1939 British history and a wide-ranging selection of primary source material.

Already published

Alan Booth   *British economic development since 1945*

Stephen Brooke   *Reform and reconstruction: Britain after the war, 1945-51*

Kevin Jefferys   *War and reform: British politics during the Second World War*

Ritchie Ovendale   *British defence policy since 1945*

Scott Lucas   *Britain and Suez: the lion's last roar*

Harold L. Smith   *Britain and the Second World War: a social history*

Forthcoming

Stuart Ball   *The Conservative Party, 1940-92*

John Bayliss   *Anglo-American relations: the rise and fall of the special relationship*

Steven Fielding   *The Labour Party: Socialism and society since 1951*

Rodney Lowe   *The classic welfare state in Britain*

Documents in Contemporary History

Britain and European integration since the Second World War

Edited by
Sean Greenwood
Reader in Modern History, Canterbury Christ Church College

Manchester University Press
Manchester and New York
Distributed exclusively in the USA and Canada by St. Martin's Press

Published by Manchester University Press
Oxford Road, Manchester M13 9NR, UK
and Room 400, 175 Fifth Avenue, New York, NY 10010, USA

Distributed exclusively in the USA and Canada
by St. Martin's Press, Inc., 175 Fifth Avenue, New York,
NY 10010, USA

British Library Cataloguing-in-Publication Data
A catalogue record for this book is available from the British Library

Library of Congress Cataloging-in-Publication Data applied for

ISBN   0 7190 4271 2   *hardback*
     0 7190 4272 0   *paperback*

First published 1996

00 99 98 97 96   10 9 8 7 6 5 4 3 2 1

Printed by Bell and Bain Ltd, Glasgow

Contents

Acknowledgements

I am most grateful to the generosity of my colleague in the Department of History at Canterbury Christ Church College, Dr Kevin Ruane, for invaluable help with the documentation covering the European Defence Community and similarly to my research student, James Ellison, for material on the Free Trade Area proposal.

For permission to publish copyright material I would like to thank the following: the Controller of Her Majesty's Stationery Office for Crown copyright material from the Public Record Office, London, the Official Report of the House of Commons Debates, Command Papers and extracts from volumes of *Documents on British Policy Overseas* (1.1–6, 1.8, 1.11, 1.15–17, 1.19, 2.3–7, 2.9–12, 2.14–18, 2.21, 2.24–26, 3.1–4, 3.6–15, 3.17, 3.19–24, 4.2, 4.4–9, 4.11–13, 4.15, 4.16, 5.1, 5.4, 5.6, 5.16, 5.17, 6.12, 6.17); Walter de Gruyter and Co. for extracts from W. Lipgens and W. Loth, *Documents on the History of European Integration, Volume 3* (1.10, 1.12, 1.20); BBC Worldwide Limited for material reproduced from M. Charlton, *The Price of Victory* (3.12, 5.3); Macmillan and HarperCollins Publishers Limited for the use of passages from Harold Macmillan, *Pointing the Way 1959–61* (4.3, 4.9, 4.10, 5.2); Curtis Brown for extracts from Tony Benn, *Against the Tide, Diaries 1973–76*, © Tony Benn 1989 (6.2, 6.5, 6.6); David Higham Associates for items from Barbara Castle, *The Castle Diaries, 1964–70, 1974–76* (5.12, 6.3); HarperCollins Publishers Limited and Peters, Fraser and Dunlop for material from Roy Jenkins, *European Diary 1977–81* and *A Life at the Centre* (6.4, 6.7, 6.8); Transworld Publishers Limited and Peters, Fraser and Dunlop for references from Nigel Lawson, *The View from Number 11: Memoirs of a Tory Radical*, published by Bantam Press, © 1992, all rights reserved (6.9, 6.14, 6.18); HarperCollins Publishers Limited for extracts from Margaret Thatcher, *The Downing Street Years* (6.10, 6.13, 6.15, 6.16); Weidenfeld and Nicolson for material from Evelyn Shuckburgh,

Acknowledgements

Descent to Suez: Diaries 1951–56 and Nicholas Henderson, *Mandarin: The Diaries of an Ambassador 1969–1982* (2.19, 2.22, 2.27, 6.1); Librairie Arthème Fayard for material from Jean Monnet, *Memoirs* (1.14, 2.1); and A. M. Heath for the extract from George Orwell, *Collected Essays, Journalism and Letters Volume IV*, © the estate of the late Sonia Brownell Orwell and Martin Secker and Warburg Ltd (1.13). Every attempt has been made to seek the permission of copyright holders, and apologies are offered to those who, inadvertently, are unacknowledged.

Without the constant support of Deborah, work on this book would have been less of a pleasure and it is lovingly dedicated to her.

Chronology of events

1945

May — Official end to the war in Europe.
United Nations Organisation set up at the San Francisco Conference.

July — Labour victory in the general election. Ernest Bevin becomes Foreign Secretary.

15 August — Official end to the war in the Far East.

1946

January–March — Fears of Soviet threat to Greece, Turkey and Iran.

February — Fear of Communist coup in France.

November — Agreement to merge the British and American zones of occupation in Germany.

1947

March — Anglo-French Treaty of Dunkirk.
Declaration of the Truman Doctrine.

June — Announcement of the Marshall Plan.

1948

January — Bevin's 'Western Union' speech.

February — Communist coup in Prague.

March — Signing of the Brussels Treaty.

April — Organisation for European Economic Co-operation (OEEC) set up to administer Marshall Aid.

June — Start of the Berlin blockade.

1949

April — North Atlantic Treaty Organisation (NATO) formed.

May — Council of Europe set up.

September — Federal Republic of Germany created.

October — German Democratic Republic created.

Chronology of events

1950
May — Schuman Plan announced.
June — Start of Korean War.
October — Pleven Plan announced.

1951
April — European Coal and Steel Community (ECSC) created.
October — Churchill re-elected as Prime Minister.

1952
May — European Defence Community (EDC) Treaty signed by the six ECSC states.

1954
August — French Assembly rejects the EDC Treaty.
October — West European Union (WEU) formed.
December — Treaty of association between Britain and the ECSC.

1955
April — Eden succeeds Churchill as Prime Minister.
June — Messina conference.
July — Spaak Committee set up to investigate means of developing European integration.

1956
March — Spaak Committee proposes a European common market.
October–Nov. — Suez crisis.
November — Macmillan announces free trade area (FTA) proposal.

1957
January — Macmillan succeeds Eden as Prime Minister.
March — Meeting between Macmillan and President Eisenhower which reasserts the 'special relationship'.
The Treaty of Rome sets up the European Economic Community (EEC) and Euratom.
October — The Maudling Committee attempts to negotiate a FTA with the EEC.

1958
December — France calls an end to the Maudling Committee negotiations.

Chronology of events

1959
January   EEC comes into operation.

1960
January   European Free Trade Association (EFTA) set up.
May   Collapse of East–West summit meeting.

1961
August   British application to join the EEC.

1962
December   Meeting between Macmillan and President Kennedy at Nassau. Polaris agreement.

1963
January   De Gaulle vetoes British membership of the EEC.

1964
October   Harold Wilson becomes Prime Minister.

1966
May–July   The Six negotiate agreement on the Common Agricultural Policy (CAP).

1967
May   Britain applies a second time for membership of the European Community (EC).
November   Sterling devalued.
De Gaulle vetoes British membership.

1969
April   De Gaulle resigns as President of the Fifth French Rebublic.

1970
June   Heath begins negotiations for British entry to the EC.

1972
January   Negotiations for British entry to the EC concluded.

1973
January   Britain formally joins the EC.

1974
March   Labour government seeks renegotiation of terms of entry.

Chronology of events

1975
March   Renegotiation completed.
June   Referendum accepts British membership of the EC.

1976
March   Callaghan succeeds Wilson as Prime Minister.
September   EC heads of government agree to direct elections to the European Parliament. Elections to be held in 1978.

1977
November   Direct elections postponed throughout the Community because of Britain's failure to meet the timetable.

1978
July   Helmut Schmidt and Giscard d'Estaing propose the establishment of the European Monetary System (EMS).
October   Callaghan decides that Britain will not participate fully in the EMS.

1979
May   Thatcher becomes Prime Minister.
June   First direct elections to the European Parliament. British budget contributions to the EC raised at the Strasbourg European Council.

1981
January   Greece becomes a member of the EC.
November   Genscher–Colombo Plan on further European integration.

1984
February   Altiero Spinelli's draft Treaty on European Union accepted by the European Parliament.
June   Agreement on British budget contributions reached at Fontainebleau European Council.
                 British paper on 'Europe – the Future' paved the way for a European Single Market.

1985
March   EC agrees on a Single Market by December 1992.
September   Inter-governmental conference (IGC) on institutional reform of the EC.

1986

January — Spain and Portugal become members of the EC.

1988

June — The Delors Committee is set up to investigate steps towards monetary union.

September — Margaret Thatcher's Bruges speech.

1989

April — The Delors report proposes three-stage progress towards EMU.

June — The Madrid European Council accepts that phase 1 of the Delors Plan – alignment of currencies within the Exchange Rate Mechanism (ERM) – should take place by July 1990.

September–Dec. — Collapse of Communism in Eastern Europe.

December — Agreement on an IGC to set a timescale for monetary union.

1990

April — A second IGC agreed to investigate political union.

October — Reunification of Germany.
Britain joins the ERM.
The Rome European Council agrees on phase 2 of the Delors Plan – the transition towards a central bank – being implemented by 1994.

November — Major succeeds Thatcher as Prime Minister.

1991

December — The European Council at Maastricht discusses the work of the two IGCs and agrees upon a Treaty on European Union.

1992

June — A Danish referendum rejects the Maastricht Treaty.

September — Financial crisis forces Britain out of the ERM.
Britain delays the process of ratification in the face of objections from Conservative 'Euro-sceptics'.

1993

January — The Single Market comes into operation.

May — Denmark accepts Maastricht in a second referendum after securing 'opt-outs' from the Treaty.

July — Britain ratifies the Maastricht Treaty.

November — The EC officially becomes the European Union.

Introduction

The fifty years since the end of the Second World War have seen the transformation of Britain from a world power to the reduced role as a partner, albeit an influential one, in a co-operative regional community of European states. Strong and persisting memories of a different historical experience have ensured an uneasy passage for this transition. Indeed, a complete adjustment to an altered status has yet to take place. The purpose of this book is to provide some insight, through a range of documentary extracts, into the attitudes and arguments associated with this convoluted process. As yet, no distinct 'schools' of historians have emerged to challenge or defend the accepted academic orthodoxy that Britain's decision to join the European Community was the right one but came too late. What historians question is at what point that error of timing could realistically have been avoided. Debate, in other words, remains centred on the detail rather than the broad sweep of events. These matters of interpretation are dealt with below and in the introductions to the extracts.

The usual warnings apply. The extracts chosen come to us principally through the focus of a particular pair of eyes – often those of people directly influencing the making of policy – and the need to be aware of the inevitable slant in these personal contributions is obvious. But official records, while enormously enriching our view of the past, also pass through some form of editing procedure before becoming a piece of raw evidence, and they too are not immune to bias. Added to this, the period covered here is a long one for a relatively slight text and this has added further to the process of selection. Subjective sources have been subjectively selected.

Subjectivity has also entered the structure of the book. It will be noted, for instance, that the treatment afforded these years is uneven, with less space given to more recent events than to the years up to the 1960s. There is a reason for this. It reflects a particular view of the way in which the historian operates and how historical judgements are arrived at – a view which, again, is neither objective nor unassailable. Despite the availability of material for this later period in the form of published private diaries and memoirs of the participants and official papers and reports, this view holds, there remains a considerable gap in the record. This makes any examination of these most recent events drift towards the art of political journalism and, while this is a respectable and necessary pursuit, it is not history. The thirty-year rule governing the release of an enormous archive of Cabinet, Treasury and Foreign Office records as well as collections of personal papers in the Public Record Office in London not only adds abundantly to the quarry in which the contemporary historian must work, it can also shift our perception of the decision-making processes of the years embraced by the rule. Our view of the attitudes and activities of Ernest Bevin, Winston Churchill, Anthony Eden and Harold Macmillan towards European co-operation has been considerably revised by the work of those historians who have had access to recently available material, and I have therefore given emphasis to these. The approach to Europe of those governments from Edward Heath's to John Major's, on the other hand, have not yet come under such scrutiny, and while it is possible for assessments to be made they must remain interim ones.

Diaries, memoirs and reminiscences, a central source for the late 1960s onwards, will not, of course, become valueless once the Public Record Office has divulged its secrets. Nevertheless, without the official record to set them against, our view of the events they describe must remain flawed. The direct and detailed political diaries of Richard Crossman, Barbara Castle and Tony Benn possess an irresistible immediacy in the absence of related Cabinet minutes.[1] But because these diarists have drafted their

---

[1] Those referred to in this volume include Richard Crossman, *Diaries of a Cabinet Minister*, London, 1975; Barbara Castle, *The Castle Diaries, 1964–70*, London, 1984; Tony Benn, *Against the Tide, Diaries 1973–76*, London, 1990.

accounts from a particular perspective and often with an eye to publication, we are looking at events through a distorting lens. Similar problems are also latent within the political memoir. These products of self-justification have long been a key ingredient in the writing of history. Indeed, their importance is sometimes most noticeable in their absence. The reluctance of Edward Heath, for instance, and many of his Cabinet colleagues to commit much to paper once out of office has caused many an historian to give thanks to the voluminous diaries of the previous Labour Cabinets, whatever imperfections these might have. In contrast, the trend which has developed since the late 1980s for virtually every ex-Cabinet minister to offer their own version of events has added copiously to the mound which the historian must excavate. But more information does not necessarily mean more enlightenment. Sometimes tediously uninformative, almost invariably self-serving, these reminiscences all lack the leaven of the wider context in which such personalised accounts need to be placed, leaving a distinct impression of being let into only part of the story – which is, of course, the case. The conflicting accounts presented by the memoirs of Nigel Lawson and Margaret Thatcher, for example, allow certain aspects of the British approach to integration in the late 1980s to be constructed with some confidence. The picture, however, can approach final definition only when tested against that range of information which is now available for the period from the 1940s through to the early 1960s.[2]

II

Throughout much of its history, Britain's interest in Europe has been closely connected with defence. Treaties were signed with the Continental states, and arrangements made with them, in order to stave off the possibility of invasion or to ensure that no single power was able to put itself in a position to invade. It should come as no surprise, therefore, that for some time after 1945 British interest in European co-operation was entangled

---

[2] Nigel Lawson, *The View from Number 11: Memoirs of a Tory Radical*, London, 1993; Margaret Thatcher, *The Downing Street Years*, London, 1993.

with aspects of defence. Early interest in co-operation with Europe, for example, sprang from a desire within the Foreign Office for what was called a 'Western bloc' of European states under British leadership as a way of hemming in post-Hitler Germany. It was Ernest Bevin, Foreign Secretary in the first post-war Labour government, who translated this rather conventional notion of a series of defence pacts with Britain's neighbours on the Continent into a wider vision which looked forward to co-operation on economic and, ultimately, political fronts.[3]

The records show that the picture we used to have of Bevin as the anti-Communist Atlanticist working assiduously to entice the Americans into defending Western Europe from the Soviet Union has been considerably overdrawn. What he wanted, rather, was a British-led 'third force' standing independently between capitalist USA and communist USSR. The base for this was to be Western Europe. This came to include a dream of 'Euro-Africa', in which the resources of the colonial empires of the Europeans would propel what he called 'the middle of the planet' – Europe and its overseas territories from Arctic Norway to the Cape of Good Hope – into the superpower league (documents 1.3 and 1.8).[4]

In a way, Bevin foreshadowed the beliefs of the European federalists such as Jean Monnet, perhaps the leading proponent of integrationist ideas in the 1950s, in his assumption that economic co-operation should come before political collaboration. But, in the end, traditional concerns for defence dominated. By 1948 the threat from a revived Germany had been overtaken by fear of Soviet expansion. Bevin's notional 'third force' was too weak to defend itself and Britain too economically dilapidated to provide it with the impetus for take-off. Like it or not, Bevin was forced to look for support to the United States. The outcome was the North Atlantic Treaty of 1949, which had more in common with the Foreign Office's 'Western bloc' than Bevin's flight of fancy into 'Euro-Africa'.[5]

---

[3] Sean Greenwood, *Britain and European Co-operation Since 1945*, Oxford, 1992, pp. 7–17.
[4] John Kent, 'The British Empire and the origins of the Cold War', in Anne Deighton (ed.), *Britain and the First Cold War*, London, 1990. Hereafter documents are referred to by number only, e.g. (1.2).
[5] John Baylis, *The Diplomacy of Pragmatism: Britain and the Formation of NATO, 1942–49*, London, 1993.

Coincidentally with Bevin's declining interest in co-operation with the Western Europeans, the road to European integration began to open. In May 1950 the Schuman Plan sketched the concept of the pooling of European coal and steel resources, which was intended to bond France and Germany pacifically together and also to provide the basis for wider European integration. British participation was on offer, but Bevin rejected it. With hindsight, this was a mistake, though an understandable one. There was little reason to believe the French plan, dependent on the improbable evaporation of traditional Franco-German rivalry, was any more substantial than his own aborted schemes. Moreover, with Britain the pre-eminent producer of coal and steel in Western Europe there was little economic enticement either (1.16–20).

Churchill's return to power in 1951 changed nothing. The new Prime Minister had assertively promoted European unity while in opposition. His ringing public speeches at Zurich and The Hague and his foundation of the United Europe Movement played an important part in the creation of the Council of Europe, which was viewed by federalists as an embryonic European Parliament. However, like Bevin after 1949, he saw the Commonwealth and close association with the United States as the foundations for British influence in the world. Though he had criticised the Labour government for not participating in the discussions which were to lead to six states (France, West Germany, Italy, Belgium, The Netherlands and Luxembourg) forming the European Coal and Steel Community, he did not alter British policy once he returned to office in 1951.[6]

It was a disappointing stance to those who had expected a more positive approach from Churchill. Among these was a group of Conservative MPs who were under the triple illusion that Churchill was interested in developing close co-operative links with Europe, that the preceding Labour government had failed to try to give a British lead, and that co-operation could take place without infringing British sovereignty (2.6–8). Churchill's inaction was put down to his having been suborned by his supposedly anti-European Foreign Secretary, Anthony Eden.

[6] John W. Young, *Britain and European Unity, 1945–1992*, London, 1993, pp. 38–9.

In fact, Eden's position on Europe was not dissimilar to Churchill's or to that of the Labour government by 1951 (2.4 and 2.5). This was, that if the Western European states wished to embark upon co-operative ventures then these should not be opposed, but Britain could not be expected to participate. Not only was this was a reflection of the British perception that its primary interests lay elsewhere, it also demonstrated a deep suspicion of the prospect of political integration which lay behind the schemes now emerging on the Continent. Eden grasped more clearly than did his parliamentary colleagues that, with federalism on a rising curve in Western Europe, closer co-operation was not open to Britain without some loss of sovereignty. Supranationalism was a marked feature both of the Schuman Plan and of the European issue which was to tax Eden the most – the proposal for the European Defence Community (EDC).

A good deal of attention has been given to this episode in the documentary sections which follow. This may seem perverse given that the EDC was the most spectacular failure of the initiatives towards integration in the post-war period. Put forward in 1950 as a way of rearming West Germany without alarming its neighbours, it was accepted in May 1952, after tortuous negotiation, by the same six states that had joined the Coal and Steel Community. Further intricate discussions before ratification of this agreement led, frustratingly, to its rejection by the French Assembly in the summer of 1954. Yet this defunct initiative has much to tell us. It demonstrates the tight connection in British thinking between Western defence and European integration. It also provides the gauge of Eden's convictions on European integration. Throughout the long and complex process he maintained a remarkable consistency. He could not contemplate the reduction in British sovereignty which joining the EDC would entail. Nevertheless, he wished it to succeed, remained doubtful that it would, and was reluctant to precipitate its collapse by offering any premature alternative (2.13). This may not have been a particularly inspiring approach, but it matched completely the attitude of the 1950–51 Labour government – and of Churchill – in its benign detachment from the integrationist aspirations of the Western Europeans. The ultimate collapse of the EDC is significant too because it reinforced the British propensity to believe that the federalist route to integration had been a false start. When the Six met at Messina, less than a year after the French had rejected the EDC, to investigate ways of extending their co-operation, the British were not inclined to take this seriously.

Even without the experience of the EDC, there were no obvious reasons for Britain to participate in the customs union which the Six decided to construct after Messina. It has been pointed out that:

> whereas most of [the Western European states] did most of their trade within Europe, Britain did most of hers outside. This made it much more rational for the countries of the continent to unite economically than it was for Britain to join them: the fact [was] that they were forming their 'common market' out of the area that was their majority market anyway, whereas Britain's majority market lay elsewhere.[7]

If we add to this the, not unrealistic, feelings that the French and Germans would find it impossible to work together, that France – the leader of the federalist cause – seemed played out as a major power, and that the Europeans would eventually swing into line behind the most prestigious state in Western Europe, the British position was far from illogical.

An important change is discernible towards the end of 1955. Though Britain accepted an invitation to join the Six in their discussions in Brussels, and could hardly have done otherwise given Churchill's condemnation of Labour's refusal to participate in the Schuman Plan deliberations, the British did so in order to guide the talks along lines acceptable to themselves. Again, this was not an unreasonable stance to take. But when, by December 1955, attempts to divert the Six looked unpromising, the British representative was withdrawn and moves were taken to wreck the unanimity of the Six (3.6). Until this point, Britain's attitude had been one of remote benevolence. Now the feeling was growing that the customs union which the Six envisaged might come to something after all and that, if it did, it was likely to be

---

[7] Bernard Porter, *Britain, Europe and the World 1850–1986: Delusions of Grandeur*, London, 1987, p. 125.

dominated by an economically rejuvenated Germany. Mixed in with fears of being on the wrong side of a discriminatory trading bloc were concerns about the security of a Europe dominated once again by Germany. In these circumstances, the British felt compelled to act.

In November 1956, almost a year on from their withdrawal from the Brussels talks, the British proposed the creation of a free trade area (FTA) in Western Europe (3.9). This marked a further shift in attitude and a recognition in London that some kind of initiative towards Europe was necessary. Unlike the proposed common market of the Messina states, the FTA was intended to exclude agricultural products and to regulate trade between member states without the imposition of a common external tariff. This meant that the British system of farming subsidies and preferential trade with the Commonwealth would be unaffected. Moreover, the FTA would have no supranational or federalist strings.

Motives behind the FTA were mixed. Essentially it was seen as a complement to the common market, an economic club for those who felt unable to join the Six. There were genuine fears too that the objectives of the Six were likely to divide Western Europe at a time of worldwide political instability and that a non-discriminatory trade arrangement between the FTA and the Six would preserve that unity in Western Europe which the Messina states seemed prepared to threaten. But there were times too when the FTA was viewed by those who proposed it more destructively as a means of enticing the lesser members of the Six away from the developing Franco-German axis and creating an alternative grouping under British influence (3.19).

This was clearly how the Six, and especially the French, saw it and they had little inclination to favour an arrangement which would give the British the best of all worlds and run the risk of sapping the essential nature of the structure they wished to create. The fundamental differences between the two sides emerged in formal talks which took place between October 1957 and November 1958, with Reginald Maudling negotiating for Britain. For a time, the British hope remained that the Six might fail to ratify the Treaty of Rome, which they had signed in March 1957. But, if anything, persisting apprehensions that British aims were destructive helped galvanise the process of ratification. Relations between Britain and France, already blighted by the Suez crisis, were made more complex by the return of General de Gaulle to power in May 1958. It soon became clear to the British that de Gaulle was determined to strengthen the Franco-German core of the nascent European Economic Community (EEC). In November, he called a halt to the proceedings of the Maudling negotiations, setting a Gaullist pattern which was to persist over the next nine years.[8]

In retrospect, of course:

> the failure to sign the Treaties of Rome was a serious mistake. In refusing to join, British governments were weakening the nation more than defending its sovereignty.... Economically and politically Britain's role became increasingly peripheral and benefits from not having joined the Communities were reduced to no more than the preservation of that same illusion of independence which led to the mistake in the first place.[9]

But we possess the knowledge, an imponderable that British policy makers could only grapple with in the 1950s, that the European Community is an economically successful permanency. We know that ten years after 1957 the bulk of Britain's imperial possessions had achieved independence. When the Treaty of Rome was signed, however, Harold Macmillan's 'wind of change' speech, which acknowledged the thrust of decolonisation, was still three years off. Banking on the 'special relationship' with the USA also turned out to be a misjudgement, and no one was more culpable in this than Macmillan – who also happened to be the most ardent protagonist of the FTA. Suez should have rung more warning bells than it did about the value of Atlanticism. On the other hand, at the peak of the Cold War, it might easily seem that Anglo-American links were symbiotic – one indication being the survival of the nuclear partnership between the two beyond the Suez crisis. Like the blind man with the elephant, the British in the late 1950s groped in the dark to put the unfamiliar creature in

[8] Derek W. Urwin, *The Community of Europe: A History of European Integration Since 1945*, London, 1995, pp. 101–15.
[9] Alan S. Milward, *The European Rescue of the Nation State*, London, 1994, p. 433.

9

Brussels into the context of a more recognisable world and it seems unnecessarily harsh for those equipped with the sharper vision of hindsight to be overly critical of their errors.

The British, then, were engaged in a process of self-education. But they proved to be slow learners. Having failed to woo the Six with the FTA, they proceeded to set up a carbon copy in the shape of the seven-strong European Free Trade Association (EFTA).[10] This was partly the product of pique, though it was also hoped that it might act as a 'bridge' to some form of association with the EEC (4.3). This was an important aspect of EFTA and, despite public assertions that the grouping of the seven states had its own economic justification, it was privately admitted that Britain's new partners' 'commercial need to come to terms [with the Six] is so great that we could not rely upon the Seven remaining in being indefinitely if there was no Seven/Six agreement.'[11]

But EFTA was hardly likely to succeed where the FTA had failed. Significantly, at the end of 1959, it became clear that the United States regarded EFTA as a complicating irrelevancy. Although the economic threat to Britain from the EEC remained a powerful consideration, the political consequences of being outside the Community now became uppermost. As the Foreign Secretary, Selwyn Lloyd, put it: 'If, of course, the Six developed into a Federal State it would become an important country and the danger might be that the Americans would pay considerably more regard to the United States of Europe than to the UK'.[12] This was crucial for it was fundamental that 'our links with the United States were more important than any other links that we might or might not have under consideration'.[13] It was this determination not to lose favour with the United States which was the principal motive behind the decision, early in 1961, to seek membership of the EEC.

Of course, the interests of the Commonwealth had to be squared with British membership. So too did the interests of the

[10] The EFTA countries were Britain, Norway, Sweden, Finland, Iceland, Austria and Switzerland.

[11] Public Record Office, London, CAB 134/1818, EQ(59)4, memorandum by the Chancellor of the Exchequer, 6 November 1959.

[12] Public Record Office, London, PREM 11/2679, summary of a meeting at Chequers, 29 November 1959.

[13] *Ibid.* Statement by the Foreign Secretary and Chancellor of the Exchequer.

British agricultural community and those of the EFTA states. Attempting to protect the interests of each of these was to colour, to a greater or lesser extent, the negotiations for British entry. The Commonwealth was an emotional issue for the British. But, as a source of cheap foodstuffs, it also presented them with a severely practical problem if these commodities were to face an external tariff. Alongside this was the question of the Common Agricultural Policy (CAP), which was being worked out by the Six as negotiations with Britain proceeded. If the CAP was accepted, it would mean a radical change in the way British farming was subsidised and a significant British contribution to subsidising the less efficient farmers in the Community. Despite these concerns, Macmillan's political skill ensured that he went forward with a united Cabinet behind him. However, the protracted negotiations which began in October 1961 soon caused cohesion in the country to dissolve.

De Gaulle played an important part in the process of delay. Exactly when the General decided to veto the British application remains open to conjecture. The French played their cards close to their chests before and during the negotiations (5.1 and 5.2). Little wonder then that Macmillan's confidence in being able to deal with the French leader shifted erratically. The one inducement available to him, considered since at least the end of 1959, was the provision of nuclear technology. Indeed, it may be that de Gaulle believed this had been offered to him and the Anglo-American Polaris deal, which emerged immediately before the 1963 veto, precipitated an act of Gaullist pique.

Macmillan's attempt to respond to changing circumstances and the deftness with which he initially moulded opposing and hesitant opinion to his purposes provoke admiration. The fact remains, however, that he also made serious errors of judgement. Though he was aware from the start that a speedy negotiation was the key to success, he has some responsibility for the extended discussions which allowed domestic opposition to crystallise and gave de Gaulle an excuse to call the negotiations to a halt (5.3 and 5.4). It was, after all, Macmillan who had been behind the creation EFTA, which added a skein of complications to the talks with Brussels. It was he who provided, via the decision to negotiate on *terms* of entry, an opening for the Commonwealth, agricultural interests and the right wing of the

Conservative Party to barrack the negotiations. Moreover, he embarked upon negotiation with the EEC without having been able to obtain from the Americans that vital concession of an independent nuclear capacity for France and without which, he knew, de Gaulle was unlikely to look favourably upon a British application. He remained, nonetheless, intermittently optimistic that he could win the General over. But the nuclear sweetener was dependent upon American approval and this was not forthcoming. Here was the most telling aspect of the application. Fundamentally, Macmillan was less interested in joining Europe than in maintaining the Anglo-American axis. Ironically, the catalyst for the British application, the preservation of the 'special relationship', was itself a prime cause of its failure.

It is no coincidence that success in the third British bid to join the European Community, in 1972, came under a Prime Minister, Edward Heath, who was lukewarm towards the 'special relationship' with the United States. Though fortunate that he did not have to face the insurmountable obstacle of de Gaulle, who left office in 1969, Heath was also unique among his predecessors and successors in possessing a commitment to the European ideal (5.14).[14] This is not to imply that without Heath Britain would have stayed aloof from Europe. The preceding Labour government, led by Harold Wilson, had applied for membership, only to be thwarted a second time by de Gaulle in 1967, and it was only Wilson's unexpected defeat in the general election of 1970 which prevented Labour making Britain's third application. Though Wilson's motives were predominantly economic and not entirely parallel to Macmillan's, the objective remained the same: to prevent further British decline. This, of course, was Heath's intention too, though it was coupled with an enthusiasm for Europe absent both before and since in a British leader.

Heath's relations with his European colleagues were not trouble free after Britain joined the Community.[15] But it was Wilson, after his return to power in 1974, who reverted to a half-resentful, semidetached condescension towards Europe, which

[14] John W. Young, *The Heath Government and British Entry into the European Community*, Leicester, 1995.
[15] See Stephen George, *An Awkward Partner: Britain in the European Community*, Oxford, 1990, pp. 60–9.

has remained the characteristic British position. Wilson's decision to renegotiate the terms of entry and hold a referendum on British membership was followed by the scepticism of his successor, James Callaghan, towards a Franco-German plan for monetary union (6.3–6). By then the frustration of the Europeans was patent. In 1978 the British ambassador in Paris noted that, 'our leading European partners were fed up with us – with our reluctant Europeanness; and they are determined to go ahead in creating a new monetary system for the Community. We would not be able to divide or break them even if should we wish to do so.'[16]

Similar advice was no doubt offered to Margaret Thatcher, whose instincts on Europe were – with the exception of Heath – entirely compatible with her predecessors'. Thatcher's private misfortune was that her fervent resistance to further integration coincided with the most vigorous impetus towards European unity since 1955. This, and her stridently assertive style, created enemies in Europe and at home, which was to be fatal to her political future (6.14–16). Though John Major had little enthusiasm for integration, one lesson from Thatcher's experience was that the European question could have disastrous personal ramifications. With a much smaller parliamentary majority than Thatcher following the election of 1992 and presiding over a party which was deeply divided over Europe, Major veered from asserting Britain's European credentials to claiming to be a bulwark against federalism. This approach was typified by the British response to the Maastricht Treaty on European Union, with Major obtaining separate treatment for Britain on those aspects of the Treaty – the Social Chapter and monetary union – which were anathema to Conservative 'Euro-sceptics'. In July 1995 he won a convincing victory in a challenge to his leadership from a 'Euro-sceptic' within his own Cabinet, but whether he will be able to continue to walk this tightrope and avoid splitting the party, as did Wilson, or face individual catastrophe, like Thatcher, remains uncertain.

[16] Nicholas Henderson, *Mandarin: The Diaries of an Ambassador 1969–82*, London, 1994, pp. 202–3, diary entry for 23 June 1978.

1
The Labour governments and European co-operation 1945–51

The Second World War gave impetus to the idea of European unity. In many of the European resistance groups and among representatives of those governments-in-exile in London which had been unable to preserve their national independence in the face of the German onslaught, a view developed that only by the creation of some form of European federation would Europe enjoy a permanent peace. The Labour government which came to power in Britain at the end of the war had no specific platform on European co-operation. However, Ernest Bevin, Foreign Secretary from 1945 to 1951, was keen to promote policies which had integrationist implications. That his efforts had come to nothing by 1951 resulted from the complexities of international politics in the immediate post-war world, which pushed Bevin towards a European defensive arrangement with the United States. The emergence of the Schuman Plan in 1950 and Britain's refusal to participate in it meant that the impetus towards integration shifted from London and came to rest firmly across the Channel.

1.1 Duff Cooper's 'political testament'

At the end of May 1944, with Allied victory in sight, Alfred Duff Cooper, the British representative to the Free French in Algiers, wrote to the Foreign Secretary, Anthony Eden, urging that Britain take the initiative in building a Western European federation after the war. His fear was that the Western European states, while looking for a British lead, would be dismayed by British hesitancy and make their

14

own plans. Duff Cooper regarded this as the most important statement of his career – his 'political testament' – and was deeply disappointed at the apparently meagre results of his advice. In fact, his memorandum was carefully considered by Eden and was influential among advisers in the Foreign Office and possibly had some influence too on the thinking of Eden's successor, Ernest Bevin.

The conquest of the air has reduced but not eliminated the importance of geography. One glance at a map of the world should convince the observer that the nations situated on the western seaboard of Europe have interests so closely in common as to render the desirability of their mutual understanding and intimate co-operation plainly apparent. Dissension between Great Britain and France must prove as fatal to Western Europe as dissension between the states of New York and Massachusetts would prove to America.... France has for long been the most important power on the western continent of Europe, and although doubts have been expressed, there seems good reason to suppose that after the war she will recover her importance....

I submit ... that policy should be directed towards the formation of a group of the Western democracies bound together by the most explicit terms of alliance. That the nucleus of that group should be the powers that have fought and suffered together – Great Britain, France, Belgium, Holland, Norway and Denmark. There is no reason why it should not subsequently be extended to Sweden, to Portugal and Spain and to Italy....

The combined Empires of Britain, France, Holland, Belgium, Portugal and Italy cover a vast portion of the earth's surface and have an enormous population. Their resources in raw materials represent a very important part of the world's supplies of tin, rubber, iron, copper, oil and fats.

Duff Cooper later summed up his ideas in his memoirs.

I had a vision of such an alliance gradually leading to a federation of the western seaboard of Europe together with the principal Powers of the Mediterranean. Practically the whole continent of Africa was at their disposal, and they might have worked together at its development for their own benefit and for that of the

15

inhabitants. Of the three great world combines, they would eventually have become the strongest. No conflict of interest would have interfered with the bonds of blood, religion and language that would have bound these countries to the New World. An alliance, based upon equality as well as goodwill, would have bridged the Atlantic Ocean, an alliance so mighty that no power on earth would have dared to challenge it, and so at last the world might have found itself on the road to permanent peace.

Public Record Office, London, FO 371, U6594/180/70, Duff Cooper memorandum, 30 May 1944; Duff Cooper, *Old Men Forget*, London, 1953, pp. 346–7.

1.2 Thoughts on post-war Europe in the Foreign Office

Officials in the British Foreign Office were also worried that future policy towards Western Europe remained unformed and, in particular, that no response had been made to prompting from the Dutch, Belgian and Norwegian governments-in-exile that a lead would be welcomed from Britain. Their proposal for what became known as a 'Western bloc' envisaged a defensive grouping in Western Europe which would hem in post-war Germany, avoid a political vacuum which might be filled by the Soviet Union, and strengthen the proposed World Security System, which was to come into being in May 1945 as the United Nations Organisation. These conclusions, from one of many discussion papers on the subject, contain most of the basic elements of what the Foreign Office had in mind.

1. Some special arrangement between Britain, France, the Netherlands, Belgium and, if possible, Norway is of great value to British interests whatever form the World Security System assumes.

2. It will be more difficult to include Denmark and Sweden, but their co-operation is not indispensable.

3. It is indispensable that France be a party. Without her no arrangement can be made except with Norway.

16

4. The commitments should be so phrased as to buttress a world-wide security system. They should exclude political and economic machinery.

5. It is necessary also to secure the goodwill of the United States and, if possible, by means of an Atlantic System she should be linked up with the scheme.

6. Great care must be taken that such arrangements do not assume the aspect of a 'bloc' directed at the USSR.

7. The advantages to the Dominions of greater security to Britain should be stressed.

> The Russians were still viewed as important post-war partners. So too were the Americans. The fear was that both would be alienated if Britain tried to build a 'Western bloc'. The real obstacle to the 'bloc' though was the Prime Minister, Winston Churchill, who saw it as an unacceptable burden. Churchill's contempt for the lesser West European states was made clear to his Foreign Secretary, Anthony Eden, who had argued in favour of the 'bloc'.

The Belgians are extremely weak, and their behaviour before the war was shocking. The Dutch were entirely selfish and fought only when attacked and then for a few hours. Denmark is helpless and defenceless, and Norway practically so. That England should undertake to defend these countries together with any help they may afford, before the French have the Second Army in Europe, seems to me contrary to all wisdom and common sense.

Public Record Office, London, FO 371, U4102/180/70, conclusions of a memorandum by Professor Charles Webster of the Foreign Office Research Department, 11 April 1944; Churchill to Eden, 25 November 1944, in Llewellyn Woodward, *British Foreign Policy in the Second World War, Volume 5*, London, 1976, pp. 193–4.

1.3   Ernest Bevin's 'grand design'

No progress was possible while Churchill was in power. Hope for those in the Foreign Office who wished to see a more positive policy towards Europe came from Ernest Bevin, who became Foreign Secretary in the summer of

1945 following the Labour Party's sweeping electoral victory. While his Foreign Office advisers limited their ideas on Europe to a post-war military/defensive union, Bevin was interested in close economic and political co-operation too. He made this clear to his officials within weeks of taking office.

[The Foreign Secretary's] long-term policy was to establish close relations between this country and the countries on the Mediterranean and Atlantic fringes of Europe – e.g. more especially Greece, Italy, France, Belgium, the Netherlands and Scandinavia. He wanted to see close association between the United Kingdom and these countries – as much in commercial and economic matters as in political questions.

> Those who worked with Bevin at this stage began to refer to these ideas as his 'grand design'. Bevin's own term for what he had in mind was 'Western Union'. His intention was that the industrial region of the Ruhr should be removed from German control and made to underpin this 'Western Union'.

[Bevin's] view was that whatever the ultimate disposal of the territory the Ruhr industries (in particular steel and chemicals) ought to be publicly owned and an international body set up to run them in order to ensure a regulated output to fit in with the economy of other countries....

The Secretary of State's long-term objective was to make the Ruhr industries a central pivot in the economy of an eventual 'Western Union'. In this way the industries (steel and chemicals) would merge into the trade of the 'Western Union'.

Public Record Office, London, FO 371, Z9595/13/17, Foreign Office minute, 13 August 1945; FO 371, UE3689/3683/53, record of a meeting between Bevin and Treasury representatives, 17 August 1945.

1.4 Bevin and the economic basis for peace

The vigour with which Bevin outlined his vision so swiftly on taking office is remarkable. Clearly he was influenced by

18

enthusiasm in the Foreign Office for a defensive 'Western bloc'. There are also marked similarities between Bevin's ideas and those of Duff Cooper. But Bevin had been an enthusiast for economic co-operation as a foundation of peace between nations since the 1920s. In the winter of 1942 he tried to persuade Eden that a European Common-wealth, working as an economic unit under the leadership of the great powers, was the best route to post-war stability.

The achievement of collective security is not solely, or even prim-arily, a political problem and any plan which sets itself merely to secure a balance of political forces will not last. We have to find an economic basis for collective security if individual nations and peoples are to recognise that they have a stake in maintaining it.

Bevin viewed his West European scheme as part of a larger series of European economic groupings, including Eastern Europe, which would serve to regenerate the continent and preserve the peace. Shortly after becoming Foreign Secretary he unfolded this side of his vision to the American Secretary of State, James Byrnes.

[He was] deeply impressed by the fact that the whole of this region represents a single economic unit which could largely be self-supporting if the various countries were to pool their resources and eliminate the tariff barriers which at present isolate each of them in its own separate poverty.... Although the Soviet Government would no doubt view with suspicion any attempt to induce these countries to cooperate in the economic field ... every effort ought nevertheless to be made to overcome Soviet ob-jections, if it is in the interest of Europe as a whole to do so.

Public Record Office, London, Bevin papers, BEVN 3/2E, Bevin to Eden, 8 December 1942; *Foreign Relations of the United States (FRUS), 1945 II*, Washington, 1967, p. 102, Bevin to Byrnes, 24 August 1945.

1.5 Responses to Bevin's 'grand design'

It was the economic departments of government, the Treasury and the Board of Trade, which expressed the deepest scepticism towards what Bevin had in mind. To them, the Western European states were too economically dilapidated to be of much use as commercial partners. Besides, it was argued, a European customs union would conflict with economic agreements entered into with the United States and would be difficult to reconcile with Britain's economic relations with the dominions and colonial territories. These were to become familiar arguments against European co-operation and were to echo around Whitehall for the next two decades. Also, since the United Nations had been set up at the San Francisco Conference in the spring of 1945, it could be argued that even the notion of a military association with the West Europeans was now redundant. In the Foreign Office, however, as the following extract shows, Bevin's ideas did receive support.

The United Kingdom, France, Holland and Belgium and their dependent territories alone would form a large potential market and a source of many key raw materials. There was nothing in this conception that was incompatible with the San Francisco decisions and, if the World Organisation (United Nations) broke down, it would provide a possible alternative. If any of the British Dominions were to join such a group it would become a very powerful combination.... There was a tendency in the United States to consider the United Kingdom as an exhausted and rather second-rate Power. The U.S.S.R., for their part, treated us with scant consideration. If we became the recognised and vigorous leader of a group of Western Powers with large dependent territories we would gain ... weight in the counsels of the Big Three.

Public Record Office, London, FO 371, UE2504/813/53, statement by Hall-Patch, economics expert at the Foreign Office, 25 July 1945.

1.6 European co-operation as a boost to British prestige

Clearly, there was an assumption that European economic co-operation would also enhance Britain's flagging status as a power of the first rank. This, as the Foreign Office minute below suggests, was always a significant consideration.

A close association between Britain, France and the Low Countries offers up most attractive vistas such as the possibility of
establishing a) a chain of strategic bases unrivalled in the world
b) an imposing array of material force ... c) control over an
important part of the raw materials of the world.... It may also
restore us, if effective, and if we manage to become leaders of the
union, as we should do if we did not bungle it, the former status
of top dog which we have now lost to the U.S.A. and U.S.S.R.

Public Record Office, London, FO 371, Z9196/13/17, Foreign
Office minute by Hebblethwaite, 10 August 1945.

1.7   Bevin and the third 'Monroe'

The objective of maintaining British power was never far
below the surface of Bevin's desire to introduce innovation
into the European state system. This aspect began to pre-
dominate as amity between the wartime partners began to
fade and Bevin realised that Britain would have to make its
own way in an increasingly dangerous world. As early as
the end of 1945 he sensed that Britain's allies were interested less in co-operation than in consolidating their own
spheres of influence. He termed these blocs 'Monroes', a
reference to the American Monroe Declaration of 1823. If
America had its 'Monroe' and the Soviet Union was consolidating its in Eastern Europe, all the more reason for
Britain to develop a third 'Monroe' in Western Europe.

If this sphere of influence business does develop it will leave us
and France on the outer circle of Europe with our friends such as
Italy, Greece, Turkey, the Middle East, our Dominions and India,
and our colonial empire in Africa: a tremendous area to defend
and a responsibility that, if it does develop, would make our
position extremely difficult. It will be realised that the continental
side of this western sphere would also be influenced and to a very
large extent dominated by the colossal military power of Russia
and by her political power which she can bring to bear through
the Communist parties in the various countries. Meanwhile,
France would stand in a kind of intermediate position, balancing
herself against the east and out of sheer necessity resting upon us.

The future too of the German people is going to be a constant source of insecurity, and every sort of political trick will be resorted to in order to control or eliminate this eventual reservoir of power ... [Britain should thus] rely on our right to maintain the security of the British Commonwealth on the same terms as other countries are maintaining theirs and to develop, within the conception of the United Nations, good relations with our near neighbours in the same way as the United States have developed their relations on the continent of America.

Quoted in R. Edmonds, *Setting the Mould: The United States and Britain 1945–50*, Oxford, 1986, pp. 27–8.

1.8   The development of Bevin's 'Monroe'

In the summer of 1946, with tension between Britain and the Soviet Union over the future of Germany adding to existing disputes over Eastern European and Middle Eastern issues, and with relations between Britain and the United States more distant than during the war, the Foreign Secretary reaffirmed his policy towards West Europe.

It would be greatly to this country's advantage if we could establish close and permanent ties, not only with France and the other neighbouring countries in Western Europe, but with all the countries on the fringe of Europe from Greece to Scandinavia and including Italy, Spain and Portugal. If all these countries could be linked together by close economic ties the position of this country, politically as well as economically, would be enormously strengthened.

Significantly, most of Britain's prospective partners in Europe still had important colonial possessions. As Bevin's interest in building a British bloc to match those of the emerging superpowers quickened during 1946 and 1947, and as he came to realise that Britain's own economic fragility was a serious impediment to initiating a West European customs union, his thoughts increasingly turned to the creation of a larger entity based on these colonial possessions. Such a grouping would automatically dominate that slice of the globe between northern Europe and southern Africa and create a 'third force' able to act independently of the Soviet and American blocs which were now clearly emerging. A conversation between Bevin and the French Prime Minister, Paul Ramadier, in September 1947 was one of several occasions when Bevin put this forward.

[Britain and France] with their populations of 47 million and 40 million respectively and with their vast colonial possessions ... could, if they acted together, be as powerful as either the Soviet Union or the United States.... If it were possible to achieve a real common front, the two countries in unison could almost immediately occupy in the world a place equivalent to that of Russia and of the United States.

In January 1948 Bevin still gave priority to developing a European group which would allow Britain to match the authority of the Americans and the Soviets.

Provided we can organise a Western European system ... backed by the resources of the Commonwealth and the Americas, it should be possible to develop our own power and influence to equal that of the United States of America and the USSR. We have the material resources in the Colonial Empire, if we develop them, and by giving a spiritual lead now we should be able to carry out our task in a way which will show clearly that we are not subservient to the United States or the Soviet Union.

Public Record Office, London, FO 371, Z7116/65/17, minute by Bevin, 8 August 1946; FO 371, 67673/8652, record of Anglo-French talks of 22 September 1947; CAB 129/23, CP(48)6, Cabinet paper, 'The first aim of British foreign policy', 4 January 1948.

1.9 Bevin's 'Western Union' speech, 22 January 1948

In the House of Commons, on 22 January 1948, Bevin made one of his most famous public statements. It is frequently seen as a prelude to the creation of the Western alliance against the Soviet Union which emerged a year later. Certainly, the statement was made at a time of increased tension with the Soviet Union and it did include a call for 'consolidation' in the West. But the speech clearly followed the pattern of the preceding group of documents, is significant for its public use of the term 'Western Union' for the first time and, as this extract demonstrates, may be viewed as a final flowering of Bevin's 'third force' idea, with Britain and the Western European states acting in unison and independently of both superpowers.

I hope that treaties will be signed with our near neighbours, the Benelux countries, making with our treaty with France an important nucleus in Western Europe. We have then to go beyond the circle of our immediate neighbours. We shall have to consider the question of associating other historic members of European civilisation, including the new Italy, in this great conception.... We should do all we can to foster both the spirit and the machinery of cooperation.... Britain cannot stand outside of Europe and regard her problems as quite separate from those of her European neighbours.... That involves the closest possible collaboration with the Commonwealth and with overseas territories, not only with the British but French, Dutch, Belgian and Portuguese. These territories are large primary producers ... and their standard of life is capable of great development. They have raw materials, food and resources which can be turned to very great common advantage, both to the peoples of the territories themselves, to Europe and to the world as a whole.... There is no conflict between the social and economic development of those overseas territories to the advantage of their peoples and their development as a source of supplies for Western Europe.

Quoted in Allan Bullock, *Ernest Bevin: Foreign Secretary*, London, 1983, pp. 519–20.

1.10 Churchill takes the initiative on Europe

By the time of the 'Western Union' speech, the American offer of what would be known as the Marshall Plan had already effectively divided Europe in two. Bevin could no longer afford the luxury of avoiding choosing sides in the Cold War. Over-riding all this was an unfolding recognition of Britain's long-term economic weakness, which underlined Britain's inability to support its even weaker neighbours in Western Europe and emphasised its reliance on the United States. Bevin's appeal for a 'Western Union' took on a military complexion in the form of the Brussels Treaty (March 1948). A year later America and Canada joined the Brussels Treaty powers of Britain, France, and the Benelux states to create the North Atlantic Treaty Organisation (NATO) (April 1949). The 'third force' concept was rejected as unworkable and Atlanticism rather than Europeanism was the favoured policy.

In the meantime, Winston Churchill appeared to put himself in the vanguard of those who proselytised on behalf of a United States of Europe. In his most influential statement on a united Europe, made at Zurich on 19 September 1946, which not only gave encouragement to supporters of co-operation throughout Western Europe but also produced the United Europe Movement (UEM) to act as a platform for British zealots of union, Churchill gave no promises that Britain would be an integral part of his proposed structure. Also, the tone remained, as this extract shows, that of an appeal to urgent action in the face of an imminent external threat.

And what is the plight to which Europe has been reduced? Some of the smaller States have indeed made a good recovery, but over wide areas a vast quivering mass of tormented, hungry care-worn and bewildered human beings gape at the ruins of their cities and homes, and scan the dark horizons for the approach of some new peril, tyranny or terror. Among the victors there is a babel of jarring voices; among the vanquished the sullen silence of despair. That is all that Europeans, grouped in so many ancient States and nations, that is all that the Germanic Powers have got by tearing each other to pieces and spreading havoc far and wide. Indeed, but for the fact that the great Republic across the Atlantic Ocean has at length realised that the ruin or enslavement of Europe would involve their own fate as well, and has stretched out hands of succour and guidance, the Dark Ages would have returned in all their cruelty and squalor. They may still return.

Yet all the while there is a remedy which, if it were generally and spontaneously adopted, would as if by a miracle transform the whole scene, and would in a few years make all Europe, or the greater part of it, as free and as happy as Switzerland is today.... We must build a kind of United States of Europe. In this way only will hundreds of millions of toilers be able to regain the simple joys and hopes which make life worth living.

But I must give you a warning. Time may be short. At present there is a breathing-space. The cannon have ceased firing. The fighting has stopped; but the dangers have not stopped. If we are to form the United States of Europe, or whatever name or form it may take, we must begin now....

I must now sum up the propositions which are before you. Our constant aim must be to build and fortify the strength of UNO. Under and within that world concept we must re-create the European family in a regional structure called, it may be, the United States of Europe. The first step is to form a Council of Europe. If at first all the States of Europe are not willing or able to join the Union, we must nevertheless proceed to assemble and combine those who will and those who can.... In all this urgent work, France and Germany must take the lead together. Great Britain, the British Commonwealth of nations, mighty America, and I trust Soviet Russia – for then indeed all might be well – must be the friends and sponsors of the new Europe and must champion its right to live and shine. Therefore I say to you! Let Europe arise!

Winston Churchill, Zurich speech, 19 September 1946, quoted in W. Lipgens and W. Loth (eds), *Documents on the History of European Integration, Volume 3*, Berlin, 1988, pp. 663–6.

1.11   British suspicion of the federalist path to unity

Bevin condemned Churchill's pronouncements on Europe as mischief making by the Leader of the Opposition. The Council of Europe, which came into being in 1949, partly inspired by Churchill's statements, was also viewed dimly by Bevin. His objectives were now being diverted by force of circumstance into Atlanticist channels, and he was less interested in this kind of development than he might otherwise have been. Moreover, Bevin's goals had always been long term, and he viewed attempts to institutionalise a unity which did not yet exist with deep suspicion. His new priorities were spelled out in a meeting with Dean Acheson, the American Secretary of State, and Robert Schuman, the French Foreign Minister, at a meeting on 10 November 1949.

I took this opportunity to draw the attention of my colleagues to the danger to our common policy if, through ill-informed criticism at home and abroad, the United Kingdom electorate were forced to choose between association with the Commonwealth and with Western Europe and if this choice became a subject of party political debate.... A remarkable amount had been accomplished since January 1948. Great confidence had been built up between the governments of Western Europe.... [But] I must warn my colleagues that the United Kingdom – because of its overseas connections – could never become an entirely European country.... The United Kingdom was widely blamed in the United States and on the continent for not doing enough for European integration but such criticism was an over simplification and had aroused great hostility. I should do my best to keep foreign policy out of the party arena. I had refrained and would in future refrain from criticism of other countries, but I would emphasise that the continuing unity of our three countries was vital if we were to consolidate the work we had begun.

Public Record Office, London, FO 371 78023, record of meeting between Bevin, Acheson and Schuman, 10 November 1949.

1.12   Contemporary criticism of Bevin's policy

By now Bevin had come to be seen both at home and abroad as an opponent of European co-operation. To some in his own party, Bevin seemed outclassed by Churchill as a European visionary, hence these views of a member of the left of the Labour Party who was also a supporter of a federal Europe.

For some time we have been aware of the grave consequences, both to this country and to Europe, resulting from the monopoly of the United Europe idea now enjoyed by Churchill and his followers. Some of us have close contacts with the European Socialists and they all ask the same questions: 'Why does nobody but Churchill speak of a United Europe? Why do you let him pervert the one idea which brings some hope of salvation? Why doesn't the Left have its own campaign?'

The need to start such a campaign forthwith is imperative. Already the Churchill Movement is gathering to itself the support of many similar groups in Europe which, if not Socialist, include many Socialists not in themselves reactionary.... We believe that these questions must at long last be answered by the establishment of a Committee composed of Socialists, both from inside and outside Parliament, and drawn from all sections of the Party and the Movement, specially devoted to conducting a campaign for European Union or, as the French call it, a Third Force.... We feel that if such an organisation is not established in the near future, a golden opportunity will be missed both for educating public opinion in Britain and for rallying the Socialist forces in Western Europe at least. These latter, owing to the fatal tactic of the Communists, have now a real chance of reviving democratic Socialist leadership, and this will be increased if they knew that in Britain the ideas for which they fight are being actively propagated.

R. W. G. Mackay, MP, to Emanuel Shinwell, Chairman of the Labour Party Executive, 16 December 1947, quoted in Lipgens and Loth, *Documents, Volume 3*, pp. 684–5.

1.13 Bevin's policy misunderstood

Bevin's untypical reticence in publicising his ideas on European co-operation between 1945 and 1948 caused him serious problems with the left of the Labour Party, in particular the so-called 'Keep Left' Group, which included Michael Foot and Richard Crossman, and which publicly condemned Bevin in May 1947 for not attempting to build a British-led third force. The Labour Party swiftly earned itself the reputation of being against European co-operation and allowed the Conservatives to claim to be the party of Europe. The extent to which Bevin's European objectives remained unknown and misunderstood by contemporaries is revealed in these rather characteristic comments from George Orwell.

If one could somewhere present the spectacle of economic security without concentration camps, the pretext for the Russian dictatorship would disappear and Communism would lose much of its appeal. But the only feasible area is western Europe plus Africa. The idea of forming this vast territory into a Socialist United States has as yet hardly gained any ground, and the practical and psychological difficulties in the way are enormous. Still, it is a *possible* project if people really wanted it, and if there were ten or twenty years of assured peace in which to bring it about. And since the initiative would have to come in the first place from Britain, the important thing is that this idea should take root among British Socialists. At present, so far as the idea of a unified Europe has any currency at all, it is associated with Churchill.

George Orwell, 29 March 1947, *Collected Essays, Journalism and Letters, Volume IV,* Harmondsworth, 1970, p. 370.

1.14   The Schuman Plan

Practical steps towards a United States of Europe came not from Churchill, but from a declaration by the French government on 9 May 1950. This was the Schuman Plan. Named after Robert Schuman, the French Foreign Minister at the time, the Plan was largely the brainchild of Jean Monnet, who was in charge of the planning authority working towards French post-war economic reconstruction. Though Monnet had an interest in wider European co-operation, his immediate objective, as this revealing extract from Monnet's first draft of the declaration indicates, was to bind together the economies of two traditional enemies, France and Germany. This would be in France's interests and implied a low level of concern on Monnet's part for British participation. Because of this, the Plan was revealed

first of all to the Germans and to the Americans before, to
Bevin's intense displeasure, being sprung on the British.

Europe must be organised on a federal basis. A Franco-German
union is an essential element in it, and the French Government
has decided to act to this end.... Obstacles accumulated from the
past make it impossible to achieve immediately the close
association which the French Government has taken as its aim.
But already the establishment of common bases for economic
development must be the first stage in building Franco-German
union. The French Government proposes to place the whole of
Franco-German coal and steel production under an international
Authority open to the participation of the other countries of
Europe.

Jean Monnet, *Memoirs*, London, 1978, p. 295.

1.15 British reactions to the Schuman Plan

As annoyance at the way the Schuman Plan had been
announced subsided, experts in the Foreign Office began to
look at it with a more dispassionate eye. The Plan was
initially scarce on detail and British officials at first chose,
reasonably enough, to see it mainly as a means by which
West Germany might be integrated more fully into the
Western comity of nations. Because this was an objective
desired by the British government, Schuman's proposal was
judged to have clear merit. Beyond this, however, it was felt
that, as the Head of the German section of the Foreign
Office advised, Britain should be wary of treading where
the Plan showed signs of wishing to lead.

It does not seem that it can be definitely said at this stage that the
French move is a deliberate and conscious rejection of the
conception of a Western Atlantic Community. It may be that
France, with her attention excessively riveted on Germany, is
principally actuated by the desire to seek a means of resolving the
contradiction between her own declared policy in regard to
Germany and her undeclared desire to see Germany permanently
under control and indeed in subjection.

The French plan speaks only of France and Germany. But in his covering note the French Ambassador emphasises that it is designed to be a European plan. Yet he does not make it clear whether or not the participation of the United Kingdom is regarded as essential. If it is not to be essential and if economic factors do not *compel* us to come in or if we could devise some form of consultative association without full participation, the prospective close association of France and Germany would be politically attractive.... And indeed it would be worth while making a substantial economic sacrifice to achieve security in Germany. But if the United Kingdom is required to join or if economic factors prevent our staying out, British participation is likely to involve us in Europe beyond the point of no return, whether the plan involves some form of immediate Federation in Europe or whether it is 'the first step in the Federation of Europe' as the French statement puts it or whether it is merely a species of European cartel....

In any event it would be damaging to take the lead at the very outset in subjecting the plan to public criticism. It has had a good reception in many quarters including governmental circles in Germany and we cannot afford to be accused of wishing to torpedo a promising move towards Franco-German rapprochement.

Memorandum by Sir Ivone Kirkpatrick, 11 May 1950, from R. Bullen and M. E. Pelly (eds), *Documents on British Policy Overseas: Series II, Volume I: The Schuman Plan, The Council of Europe, and Western European Integration 1950–1952* (hereafter cited as *DBPO*), London, 1986, pp. 34–5.

1.16 British tactics towards the Schuman Plan

Nervous of any latent supranational elements in the Schuman Plan, yet reluctant to appear entirely negative, British officials decided upon a waiting game of refusing to be committed to initial discussions on the Plan while holding out the prospect of a non-committal association with talks between Paris and Bonn. As the following advice to Bevin suggests, an underlying feeling existed in the first days after the announcement of the Plan that the French had made a gaffe in publicising it in so nebulous a form, and that the initiative and the chance to fill in the detail still lay with London.

There has been no formal approach from the French.

The purpose of the scheme was Franco-German rapprochement, but the French have tried to negotiate with us before approaching the Germans.

They have not thought out how their scheme will work and we could not accept it in principle as we do not know what it would involve.

The French say they are prepared to go ahead with the Germans, but they have not done so, neither have they worked out their proposals any further than the communiqué.

We shall have to do what we can to get them out of the mess into which they have landed themselves.

I therefore think that M. Schuman should be informed on the following lines:

His Majesty's Government have already welcomed the initiative taken by the French Government.

There have since been some informal contacts with M. Monnet from which it has emerged that the proposals are not sufficiently developed to enable us to take a decision in principle to accept them, especially having regard to the special geographic and Commonwealth considerations which we have in mind.

We understood that a main motive was to make a fresh approach to the German proble[m], and that this desire has been reciprocated in Germany.

We had expected that the next step would therefore be to arrange for negotiations to be opened with the German Government....

We are anxious that this initiative of the French Government shall succeed. We should therefore wish to be associated in some way with the proposed authority....

Sir Roger Makins to Bevin, 19 May 1950, from Bullen and Pelly, *DBPO: Series II, Volume I*, pp. 71–2.

1.17 The Foreign Office advises rejection of the Schuman Plan

The assertion that the French had not approached the Germans was wrong. Paris had, in fact, been in touch with

Konrad Adenauer, the Federal Chancellor, on 9 May, the day the Schuman Plan was put before the French Cabinet. Moreover, this Franco-German reconciliation was not the core of the Plan, as the British were still inclined to believe, but was subservient to the notion of sector-by-sector economic integration leading to the eventual political unification of Europe. To preserve this fundamental aspect, Monnet was prepared to veto British attempts merely to be associated with discussions. Britain must be committed from the start or else excluded. This was to be a second jolt for the British and materialised in a French ultimatum on 1 June which insisted that Britain accept the Schuman proposals as a basis for negotiation within twenty-four hours. The implications were spelled out for the Cabinet by the leading civil servant in the Treasury, Sir Edward Bridges.

[The French communiqué] essentially seeks to commit us in advance of negotiations to the principle of pooling European steel and coal resources and to the surrender to an independent authority of sovereignty over an important sector of our economy. We think it wrong to commit ourselves in this way, not because we necessarily preclude any possibility of some measure of pooling or some surrender of sovereignty, but because we think it wrong to pledge ourselves on these matters without knowing more precisely the nature of the commitment we are being invited to accept.

On this basis we would, therefore, have to contemplate the prospect that the others may go ahead without us. Our provisional view is that the economic arguments in favour of coming in or staying out of an international association of the kind contemplated by the Schuman plan are not conclusive one way or the other, and on this score there need be no cause for alarm if at this stage the French decide to proceed without us.

The main issues are really political. The exchanges with the French have brought out that their proposals, which started in a Franco-German context, have now been given a wider application. It is not merely pooling of resources, but also, in the first place, the conception of fusion or surrender of sovereignty in a European system which the French are asking us to accept in principle.... It has been our settled policy hitherto that in view of our world position and interests, we should not commit ourselves irrevocably to Europe either in the political or the economic sphere unless we could measure the extent and effects of the commitment. This is in effect what we are now being asked to do....

It will be seen, therefore, that there is a real difference of view between ourselves and the French which cannot be glossed over by mere verbal ingenuity in the drafting of a communiqué, and in our view it is better to face this issue now rather than later. For the above reasons we recommend that the latest French proposal should be rejected.

Sir Edward Bridges to the Cabinet, 2 June 1950, from Bullen and Pelly, *DBPO: Series II, Volume I*, pp. 137–8.

1.18 'The great mistake of the post-war period'?

> The above judgement by the American Secretary of State, Dean Acheson, on Britain's decision to reject the Schuman Plan highlights how much of a turning point this was. Germany, Italy and the Benelux countries joined with France to create the European Coal and Steel Community (ECSC). Britain was left on the periphery of European economic co-operation for over twenty years. This was recognised by a leader writer on *The Economist* shortly after Britain's decision to say no. But the writer also acknowledged the serious impediments to British acceptance of the Plan, not only by the way in which it was presented to them, but also by the uncertainty of its success, and, above all, by its emphasis on federalism.

One can regret that the issue was brought up by such unworthy tactics. One can regret that so mighty a principle as the pooling of sovereignty was invoked, and such high hopes of permanent pacification aroused, in support of a proposal which only those versed in its formidable technicalities can really understand – and whose actual practical accomplishments may yet turn out to be small. One can be deeply distrustful of the French and American leaning to the dangerous and difficult principle of federalism, and disappointed at the failure to realise how much sovereignty has already been pooled in defence matters by much less spectacular and more workmanlike methods, in which the British have been the reverse of backward.

But when all these things have been said, the fact remains that at the bar of world opinion, the Schuman proposal has become a test. And the British Government have failed it.

The Economist, 10 July 1950.

1.19   Some unsound motives

> Of course, the Labour government's decision was not entirely rational. A proposal for European co-operation coming from the French was almost as distasteful as one coming from Churchill. Bevin was temperamentally averse to accepting attempted faits accomplis or ultimata. He was also very ill in the spring of 1950 and hospitalised at times when urgent decisions had to be made. Suspicions were sometimes expressed too, in Labour circles, that the conservative Christian Democratic governments most interested in the Schuman Plan were part of a faintly sinister conspiracy.

Officially we have welcomed the idea, and so have the Americans. So has Adenauer for the German Federal Republic. Indeed it seems clear he *was* in the know. Privately we all have our doubts and misgivings. In view of the political complexion of the French and German govts. and their links with heavy industry, one cannot but expect that this will develop along old fashioned cartel lines. It need not do so, however, and if we can get the scheme executed in a way that safeguards the public interest and limits the power of the vested interests in the international authority, then it *may* be a step forward. On the other hand it may be just a step in the consolidation of the catholic 'black international' which I have always thought to be a big driving force behind the Council of Europe.

Kenneth Younger, Minister of State at the Foreign Office, diary entry, 14 May 1950, from Bullen and Pelly, *DBPO: Series II, Volume I*, p. 35.

1.20 Essentially a logical decision

On the other hand, it seems fair to say that the British decision was based on a thorough and rational investigation of the central issues. There was keen interest in closer co-operation between France and Germany, and the British government intended to do nothing that would block this. It was not, however, judged to be worth the price of dabbling in federalism. After all, Britain in 1950 remained indisputably a world, rather than merely a regional, power. Abandoning important elements of sovereignty to European neighbours appeared perverse in the light of Britain's global and Commonwealth interests. This was the overwhelming view in the political advice given to the government. Linked with this was the fact that the Sterling bloc and the Commonwealth were more important trading partners than any West European state. Such questions were not ignored by the Labour government, and the opinion of those concerned with the industries which would be directly concerned supported the view that there was little on offer to entice the British.

R. M. Shone (British Iron and Steel Federation [employers])
... Mr. Shone felt that taking the iron and steel industry as a whole, the Commonwealth markets and preferences were more important to most sections of industry than the possibility of gaining unrestricted entry to European markets.

B. L. Evans (Iron and Steel Trades Confederation [trade union])
... From the trade union standpoint he foresaw many complexities, particularly in regard to the proposal for equalising living conditions.
Labour conditions depend upon trade union strength and government policy, and the United Kingdom enjoys the best conditions in Europe (with the possible exception of Sweden). The higher authority would have to raise the level in other countries to the United Kingdom level, and he could not see how this could be done for (say) the French steel industry in isolation from other French industries. On the Continent there is, from the trade union point of view, a closer connection than in the United Kingdom between the steel industry and other industries

(particularly the engineering industry) and selective treatment would accordingly be more difficult.

In principle British trade unionists are convinced internationalists, but it is very unlikely that they would, in practice, look with favour on a proposal to share labour's portion of the fruits of increased productivity in the United Kingdom steel industry with Continental workers whose productivity is less.

H. R. Hodgson (National Coal Board)

... The National Coal Board would be opposed to any arrangement which gave an international authority power to issue directions on the management of the United Kingdom coal industry (e.g. that a certain pit or area should be closed down) capable of affecting the balance of the whole industry.

Working Party on the Proposed Franco-German Coal and Steel Authority, minutes of the first meeting, 25 May 1950, quoted in Lipgens and Loth, *Documents, Volume 3*, pp. 744–6.

2

Out of step: Britain and the proposal for a European army 1951–54

Few expected cooperation with Europe to be very high on Britain's political agenda when Winston Churchill returned to office in October 1951. Nevertheless, the new Prime Minister's pro-European statements while in opposition did suggest that a more positive response to integration would now be discernible. As it turned out, the Churchill government adopted an approach which was identical to that of the Labour government in its later stages: to give support to co-operative schemes and to associate with them, but to avoid compromising British sovereignty by full participation. This was a disappointment to many European federalists and also to those Conservative MPs who mistakenly believed that a closer association with Europe than Churchill envisaged, but which fell short of integration, was an available option.

Meanwhile, the Foreign Secretary, Anthony Eden, tried to weave a course which would demonstrate Britain's European credentials without full commitment. This was centred on the tortuous negotiations to create an integrated European army via the EDC, which had emerged in October 1950 when Labour was still in office. Because they were doubtful of its practicality and because it involved a supranational minister of defence, the Labour government had decided to distance themselves from the project without appearing to undermine it. Again, they would not join it but would associate themselves with it. This was Eden's stance, too. Additional complexities arose from the fact that the EDC was intended not only to move integration forward, but also to provide a safe way of rearming Germany. After three and a half years of gruelling negotiations, the EDC project collapsed. The defence agreement which Eden salvaged from the wreckage was regarded as a personal triumph. In the process, however, he earned an unfair reputation as an anti-European.

2.1   Origins of the EDC

The outbreak of the Korean War in June 1950 was widely interpreted as the preliminary to a Soviet offensive in Europe. To the consternation of many Europeans, especially the French, the United States demanded the rearmament of West Germany as a means of stiffening European defences. Monnet feared that a wholly negative French stance would alienate both the Americans and the Germans and wreck the Schuman proposals, which were still being negotiated. He drafted a scheme for a fully integrated European army, controlled by a supranational minister of defence, and showed it to his political ally René Pleven, the French Prime Minister. This allowed for German forces to be controlled by Germany's neighbours. It was also intended to mark a further step towards a federal Europe.

If we let events take their course, we shall sooner or later be forced to agree to a compromise solution (priority for France, but a German army made up of small units) which will simply be an illusion. By this indirect means, the German Army will be reborn. Our resistance will have proved futile. We shall lose face, and lose the political initiative. Perhaps the Schuman Plan will be carried out, but in Bonn rather than in Paris.

Our attitude must be extremely firm, and we must resolutely oppose America's present policy. But we have no hope of succeeding unless we give our opposition a positive content inspired by an overall policy for Europe.

I am anxious to bring the Schuman Plan conference to a successful conclusion, and I therefore think I must suggest to you what seems to me the only way out of the impasse, which is to make a positive contribution to solving the German problem. Before the Defence Committee meets in New York on October 28, the French Government should:

(i)   reiterate its implacable opposition, in the interests of Europe and of peace, to the re-establishment of a German army;

(ii) propose that the solution of the German problem in its military aspect be sought in the same spirit and by the same methods as for coal and steel: the establishment of a European Army with a single High Command, a single organisation, unified equipment and financing, and under the control of a single, supranational authority (German units would gradually be integrated into this initial nucleus);

(iii) seek guarantees that this solution will not be adopted until after the Schuman Treaty is signed.

Jean Monnet, *Memoirs*, London, 1978, pp. 345–6, letter from Monnet to René Pleven, 14 October 1950.

2.2 Churchill's call for a European army

The Pleven Plan, as Monnet's improvisation came to be called, was presented to the French National Assembly on 24 October 1950. It had been pre-empted, however, in its call for a European army by a speech made at the Consultative Assembly of the Council of Europe at Strasbourg by Churchill on 11 August of the same year.

Great Britain and the United States must send large forces to the Continent. France must again provide her famous Army. We welcome our Italian comrades. All – Greece, Turkey, Holland, Belgium, Luxembourg, the Scandinavian States – must bear their share and do their best....

We should now send a message of confidence and courage from the House of Europe to the whole world. Not only should we re-affirm, as we have been asked to do, our allegiance to the United Nations, but we should make a gesture of practical and constructive guidance by declaring ourselves in favour of the immediate creation of a European army under a unified command, and in which we should bear a worthy and honourable part.

Quoted in Harold Macmillan, *Tides of Fortune 1945–1955*, London, 1969, p. 217.

2.3   The Labour government and the EDC

Initially, the Pleven Plan was viewed by the Labour government with deep distrust. It was judged to be a French attempt to put off discussions on German rearmament and to cut across British policy of tightening the Atlantic alliance. By the summer of 1951, ministers had come to see advantages in the Plan. The EDC was gaining support among the six states which were to form the ECSC. British backing for it would, it was thought, stimulate interest in European rearmament, which the government, especially since Korea, considered to be a priority. Of more importance, the EDC now found favour in Washington. Herbert Morrison, who had replaced Bevin as Foreign Secretary earlier in the year, and Emanuel Shinwell, Minister of Defence, advised the Cabinet that Britain should back the EDC but not join it.

Hitherto all N.A.T.O. negotiations on a German defence contribution have been bedevilled by the conflict between French resistance to any form of German rearmament and American insistence on the immediate need for a German contribution. This conflict has put a serious strain on the relations of the three major N.A.T.O. Powers which it is important to avoid for the future. It would be a mistake to underestimate French fears of the danger of German military revival on one hand and of action liable to provoke Russia on the other: their plan for a European Army is designed to reduce both these dangers and we consider that the only hope of securing their agreement to a German defence contribution lies in agreeing in principle that it should be made in the context of a European Army. This means that in any arrangement resulting from these discussions the United States, United Kingdom and Germany will have to give the French an undertaking that any German contribution will eventually take the form of a contribution to the European Army. We do not, of course, suggest that the United Kingdom should itself join the European Army.

Acceptance of the French thesis on this major point would also have the following advantages:

    (a) it would present German rearmament to the world at large, and to the Soviet Union in particular, in the most favourable and least provocative light possible, i.e., as part of the movement towards European unity and not as a purely military measure;

(b) it would be a further step towards integrating Germany in the West and might prove a useful half-way house to eventual German membership of N.A.T.O.;

(c) it would make the French more willing to agree to a solution of the German political problem which will enable Germany to associate herself with Western defence.

Public Record Office, London, CAB 131/11, DO(51)89, memorandum to Cabinet Defence Committee, 24 July 1951.

2.4 Labour's European policy at the end of the Attlee governments

This advice was accepted and as the second post-war Labour government moved precariously towards an autumn general election, which it was to lose, the Prime Minister, Clement Attlee, felt that policy towards the EDC encapsulated the government's overall attitude towards integration. It was an attitude which, he told the Cabinet, he wished to see publicised in order to scotch widespread claims that the government was against European co-operation.

We are willing to play an active part in all forms of European cooperation on an inter-governmental basis but cannot surrender our freedom of decision and action to any supranational authority. We are quite ready to encourage Continental countries who feel disposed to adopt such plans and in the case of the Schuman Plan have declared our wish to be closely associated with any Authority that may be set up under it. We are considering the possibility of making a more definite statement in this sense in the near future. We are also ready to look very sympathetically on the European Army Plan provided it can be shown to be militarily effective. We are anxious to develop the consultative role of the Council of Europe which is the focal point of the European integration movement.

Public Record Office, London, CAB 129/47, CP(51)239, memorandum by Attlee to the Cabinet, 30 August 1951.

2.5   The Washington Declaration

The Labour government's statement came in the shape of a joint declaration following a meeting of the Foreign Ministers of Britain, France and the United States in Washington on 14 September 1951. Less assertive in its concern for British sovereignty than were the government's internal memoranda, the Washington Declaration helped refuel hopes that Britain might, after all, make common cause with the integrationists.

The three Foreign Ministers declare that their Governments aim at the inclusion of a democratic Germany, on a basis of equality, in a Continental European Community, which itself will form a part of a constantly developing Atlantic Community.

The three Ministers recognise that the initiative taken by the French Government concerning the creation of a European Coal and Steel Community and a European defence community is a major step towards European unity. They welcome the Schuman Plan as a means of strengthening the economy of Western Europe and look forward to its early realisation. They also welcome the Paris Plan as a very important contribution to the effective Defense of Europe, including Germany.

The participation of Germany in the common defense should naturally be attended by the replacement of the present Occupation Statute by a new relationship between the three Governments and the German Federal Republic.

The Government of the United Kingdom desires to establish the closest possible association with the European continental community at all stages in its development.

The three Ministers reaffirm that this policy, which will be undertaken in concert with the other free nations, is directed to the establishment and the maintenance of a durable peace founded on justice and law. Their aim is to reinforce the security and the prosperity of Europe without changing in any way the purely defensive character of the North Atlantic Treaty Organisation. They reaffirm their determination that in no circumstances shall the above arrangements be made use of in furtherance of any aggressive action.

Joint statement by Morrison, Schuman and Acheson, Washington, 14 September 1951, from R. Bullen and M. E. Pelly (eds), *Documents on British Policy Overseas: Series II, Volume I. The Schuman Plan, The Council of Europe, and Western European Integration 1950–1952* (hereafter cited as *DBPO*), London, 1986, pp. 723–4.

2.6   The Conservative 'pro-Europeans'

Because of Churchill's reputation as a self-proclaimed supporter of European unity, the return of the Conservatives to office on 25 October 1951 added to expectations that Britain would now take the lead in Europe. This was the case not only abroad, but also in certain circles of the Tory Party. A group of Conservative MPs including Robert Boothby, Harold Macmillan and David Maxwell-Fyfe, who had been supporters of Churchill's United Europe Movement and some of whom represented Britain at the Council of Europe in Strasbourg, now urged Churchill and Eden to take the initiative in Europe. This group, as this letter from the Conservative MP Julian Amery to Harold Macmillan suggests, believed that the Labour government had never attempted co-operative policies and had damaged Britain's reputation abroad by being indefatigably anti-European, and that the Conservative government could improve this reputation by offering co-operation which fell short of federalism. These were illusions.

Dear Harold,

I was in Paris this week-end for the meeting of the General Affairs Committee. There and in private talks with Reynaud,

Mollet,[1] Palewski[2] and others, I was impressed by a general sense of despondency about the prospects of the Schuman Plan. The Dutch, as you know, are the only Parliament which has yet ratified it, and, though the others are expected to follow suit, except perhaps the Belgian, no-one any longer seems to think that the Plan itself will come to much. There is the same sort of feeling about the Pleven Plan.

It rather looks as if we are faced with precisely the situation (and the opportunity) which you envisaged last summer. The Schuman and Pleven Plans are groggy. We could still save them. It is a question of going in and making them work. Guy Mollet said he hoped we would ask for a special conference to discuss the terms on which we could go in. In his view it would not now be difficult to get both plans amended to meet our particular requirements.

Churchill's return has, certainly, created the psychological background for us to take up the leadership of Europe, and the present state of the Schuman and Pleven Plans seems to offer a practical opportunity to take the initiative. But we ought to act before the Assembly meets or at Strasbourg itself. Schuman has announced that he will make proposals for a Continental Federation at the next session of the Assembly. Reynaud looked to me as if he was bursting with some new proposal which he is going to make at the meeting with the Americans. (He gave me no idea of what it was but he harped so much on the importance of the meeting that I feel sure he has something up his sleeve.) Finally we have the Gaullists who will now be at Strasbourg for the first time with General Koenig *en tete*.[3] I understand from Palewski that, in their view, nothing can be done until a European political authority has first been constituted. All this suggests that we may be faced at Strasbourg with a series of proposals from the French side which would revive the federal issue. We should have to reject them and, unless we had put ourselves in the right by making practical proposals of our own, the cry would go up – and with some reason – that we were no better than the Socialists.

[1] French delegates to the Council of Europe.
[2] Vice-President of the French National Assembly.
[3] That is, as leader of the Gaullists at Strasbourg.

I am sorry to bother you with all this; but this is really your idea which I am trying to revive and you will know best what, if anything, can be done about it.

JULIAN AMERY

Letter from Amery to Macmillan dated 12 November 1951, and which was passed on to Eden, *DBPO: Series II, Volume I*, pp. 755–6.

2.7 Churchill's 'no'

Churchill's stance, disingenuously sweeping aside all that he had seemed to imply while in opposition, was made quite clear to the Cabinet within weeks of returning to power.

UNITED EUROPE

Note by the Prime Minister and Minister of Defence

At Zurich in 1946 I appealed to France to take the lead in Europe by making friends with the Germans, 'burying the thousand-year quarrel,' etc. This caused a shock at the time but progress has been continual. I always recognised that, as Germany is potentially so much stronger than France, militarily and economically, Britain and if possible the United States should be associated with United Europe, to make an even balance and to promote the United Europe Movement....

But I never thought that Britain or the British Commonwealth should, either individually or collectively, become an integral part of a European Federation, and have never given the slightest support to the idea. We should not, however, obstruct but rather favour the movement to closer European unity and try to get the United States' support in this work.

... On the economic side, I welcome the Schuman Coal and Steel Plan as a step in the reconciliation of France and Germany and as probably rendering another Franco-German war physically impossible. I never contemplated Britain joining in this plan on the same terms as Continental partners. We should, however, have joined in all the discussions, and had we done so not only a better plan would probably have emerged, but our own interests would have been watched at every stage. Our attitude towards further economic developments on the Schuman lines resembles that which we adopt about the European Army. We help, we dedicate, we play a part, but we are not merged and do not forfeit our insular or Commonwealth-wide character. I should resist any American pressure to treat Britain as on the same footing as the European States, none of whom have the advantages of the Channel and who were consequently conquered.

Our first objective is the unity and the consolidation of the British Commonwealth and what is left of the former British Empire. Our second, the 'fraternal association' of the English-speaking world; and third, United Europe, to which we are a separate closely- and specially-related ally and friend.

Public Record Office, London, CAB 129/48, C(51)32, 29 November 1951.

2.8   Eden the 'anti-European'

> It was Eden, however, not Churchill who received the odium of the 'pro-Europeans' in his Party. Twenty years later his reputation had crystallised into that of an unyielding opponent of co-operation.

Eden felt himself out of the European swim. He became, and the Foreign Office under him became, sincerely opposed but implacably opposed to the whole European concept, to Strasbourg and all it stood for. He once said to me, 'Association, not participation. Association is as far as I'm prepared to go in any European connection'. And rather quizzically he added, 'You see the difference between us is that you're a European animal and I'm basically an Atlantic animal'.

When the Conservative government got in, in the late autumn of 1951, hopes for the Council of Europe were raised very high. The first thing that was under consideration was the European Defence Community, and don't forget that the year before Churchill had demanded the European Army at the assembly of the Council of Europe. What happened was that David

Maxwell-Fyfe, then Home Secretary, later Lord Kilmuir, came out to Strasbourg and, representing the British government, said that although we couldn't unconditionally join the proposed European Defence Community, it was a matter of negotiation between the governments concerned, and that every method would be attempted. At a press conference afterwards, at which I was present, he said 'There's no refusal on the part of Britain'. On the same night, at a press conference in Rome, Eden, as Foreign Secretary, announced that we would not join the European Defence Community on any terms whatsoever. The Conservatives at Strasbourg sent a desperate message to Churchill, after Eden had turned down EDC, saying that we must make our goodwill known, otherwise Europe would fall apart and form something without us. It was a really strongly worded letter of protest asking if we had gone back on everything that we said. We got no reply to it at all....

Robert Boothby, Conservative 'pro-European', in Alan Thompson and John Barnes, *The Day Before Yesterday*, London, 1971, p. 104.

2.9 'An unhappy misunderstanding'[4]

The incident to which Boothby refers to above was seen by the 'pro-Europeans' as a betrayal by Eden of the new direction in British policy towards Europe which they anticipated. In reality, unless London embraced federalism there was no new course to be had. In any case, Maxwell-Fyfe's statement at Strasbourg was also open to a negative interpretation and in Rome Eden publicly reaffirmed the Washington Declaration,[5] adding, under questioning from the press, a gloss to the Declaration which clearly suggested that some form of British association with the EDC was on the cards.

Question: Does the use of the word 'association' in the September 14th Document rule out any participation of British units?

[4] Macmillan, *Tides of Fortune*, p. 463.
[5] See 2.5.

Answer: So far as British units are concerned yes. As far as *formations* are concerned yes, but there might be some other form of association. *Question:* Is the report true, which I have just heard, that Sir David Maxwell-Fyfe has just rejected the Schuman Plan. *Answer:* I haven't seen the text of Sir David's speech, but I imagine that he would have based himself, as I have, on the Declaration of 14th September which did mark a considerable advance in the British attitude towards both the Schuman Plan and the European Army.

Press conference at the end of a NATO Assembly meeting in Rome, 28 November 1951, *DBPO: Series II, Volume I,* p. 766.

2.10   The strength of federalist feeling in France

The position of the Conservative 'pro-Europeans', notably Macmillan, was based, in part, on a view that the power of the French federalists was exaggerated and that recent European co-operative developments could, therefore, be directed into channels acceptable to Britain. Eden, however, was receiving a different picture from the British embassy in Paris.

If the Schuman and Pleven Plans succeed a European community will be created with its own legislature, executive and judiciary, controlling the military and to a great extent the economic life of the communities concerned and likely in the course of time to achieve more reality that the national States which form its constituent parts. The inspiration behind all this comes largely from M. Monnet, in whose conversation the most recurrent phrase is 'the whole thing has got to be changed entirely.' M. Monnet and those who are inspired by his ideas are firmly convinced that there is nothing sacrosanct about existing institutions. If their plans succeed the army will disappear, the Assembly in the Palais Bourbon will be reduced, not at once but in due course, to the status of the legislature of New York State, and the French State, the oldest established national unity in the world, will begin the process of merging itself into another, larger, but less historic entity....

What chances has this policy of succeeding? The answer to this question depends on many factors which are outside French control and thus outside the purview of this despatch, but no doubt also much depends on the action of the French Government, parliament and people. Here there are many unpredictable factors. The French people are ill-informed on the issues involved and the sacrifices and risks which the policy would bring with it. Parliament is hopelessly divided, and the Government – any potential government – is weak. The course of action proposed involves fundamental changes in French thought and life, affecting personally the average Frenchman much more than the normal course of peacetime foreign policy can be expected to do. As I have said the French people are not conscious of this and when they do become conscious of it all sorts of resistances may be set up. Moreover, the unpredictable course of French internal policy may paralyse French foreign policy at a critical moment and let precious opportunities slip. Nevertheless on balance I think it unlikely that the policy will fail because it has been rejected by France. French parliamentarians and the French people know that it is a French policy and, however little they understand it, they are proud of it as an innovation for which France is responsible. French national pride will, in fact, be engaged in the success of the experiment. Nor are the French so attached to their own institutions as not to be prepared to sacrifice them on the altar of a new idea which seems to promise them hope for the future and fresh honour among nations. Thus, though there will be many misgivings, on the whole I expect the French parliament to approve the policy in the end. Whether they will do so in time, and whether they will be prepared to accept the sacrifices and the expenses which the policy logically involves, are other and more difficult questions.

Public Record Office, London, PREM 11/165, Oliver Harvey, British ambassador in Paris, to Eden, 5 November 1951.

2.11   Eden's European policy

Macmillan, like Churchill and Boothby, wanted to see the Schuman Plan and the EDC collapse. In contrast, Eden worked on the assumption that they would succeed, believed they were not inherently disadvantageous to Britain, and was prepared to consider the benefits that integration might bring so long as guided by formal British association with these developments. Above all, he wished to avoid any accusations of sabotage, which might offend the United States and alienate the West Europeans. His views were circulated to the Cabinet at the end of the year.

(a) The defeat and humiliation suffered by many European countries in the last war has stimulated a desire for closer integration in Western Europe.

(b) The most prominent countries in the movement are France and Germany. Both see in the movement a chance of ending their age-long rivalry. At the same time both believe that they will derive certain purely national advantages from integration.

(c) The movement is still in its infancy. Provided it does not suffer a major set-back, it should lead to an effective working union of the Schuman Plan countries, led by France and Germany.

(d) A union of the Schuman Plan countries would not be dangerous in the short term to the United Kingdom. In the long term, there is a danger that if, as is probable, Germany emerges as the predominant economic partner, she will use her position to our disadvantage both in the commercial and political field.

(e) There is also a danger, in the longer term, that a federalist union might constitute a neutral *bloc* in a world conflict.

(f) None the less, the United Kingdom cannot and should not try to divert the integration movement from its present course.

(g) Owing to her position as a World Power, the United Kingdom cannot join the integration movement. But she can and should associate herself with it in a friendly fashion.

(h) The aim of the United Kingdom should be so to guide the course of the integration movement that any continental union which emerges should take its place as a part of the wider Atlantic community.

Conclusions of a memorandum by the Foreign Office Permanent Under-Secretary's Committee on 'European Integration', 12 December 1951, *DBPO: Series II, Volume I*, p. 788.

2.12   The 'sludgy amalgam'

The EDC forced itself upon Eden as a pragmatic issue to be resolved because it provided a possible compromise to American insistence that Germany should contribute to the defence of Europe and the fears of the French, and others, of the potential consequences of an independent German army. Churchill did not see it this way and clearly preferred a 'NATO' solution to German rearmament – which France had already rejected.

There can be no effective defence of Western Europe without the Germans. As things developed my idea has always been as follows: there is the NATO Army. Inside the NATO Army there is the European Army, and inside the European Army is the German Army. The European Army should be formed by all the European parties to NATO *plus* Germany, 'dedicating' from their own national armies their quota of divisions to the Army now under General Eisenhower's command. Originally at Strasbourg in 1950 the Germans did not press for a national army. On the contrary, they declared themselves ready to join a European Army without having a national army. The opportunity was lost and there seems very little doubt that Germany will have to have a certain limited national army from which to 'dedicate'. The size and strength of this army, and its manufacture of weapons, would have to be agreed by the victorious Powers of the late war. In any case the recruiting arrangements for covering the German quota would have involved a considerable machinery.

In the European Army all dedicated quotas of participating nations would be treated with strict honourable military equality. The national characteristics should be preserved up to the divisional level, special arrangements being made about the 'tail' heavy weapons etc. I should doubt very much the military spirit of a 'sludgy amalgam' of volunteers or conscripts to defend the EDC or other similar organisations. The national spirit must animate all troops up to and including the divisional level. On this basis and within these limits national pride may be made to promote and serve international strength.

France does not seem to be playing her proper part in these arrangements. France is not France without 'L'Armée Française'. I warned M. M. Pleven and Monnet several times that 'a Pleven

Army' would not go down in France. The French seem to be trying to get France defended by Europe. Their proposed contribution for 1952 of five, rising to ten, divisions is pitiful, even making allowances for the fact that they are still trying to hold their Oriental Empire. They have no grounds for complaint against us who have already dedicated four divisions to General Eisenhower's Command. We must not lose all consciousness of our insular position.

Public Record Office, London, CAB 129/48, C(51)32, memorandum by Churchill, 29 November 1951.

2.13   Eden's approach to the EDC

> Eden had to convince Churchill and fend off his Conservative opponents. He took the pragmatic view that organisational matters were not a priority. His concern was to heal the breach which had appeared in NATO over European defence by appeasing the Americans and reassuring the West Europeans without antagonising the Soviet Union. If the EDC did, in the end, fail – as wrangling between the six states now negotiating an EDC treaty suggested that it might – then some other solution would have to be found. The danger was, in his view, to move too early. This position, outlined here to Churchill, characterised Eden's policy towards the EDC over the next two and a half years.

Thank you for letting me see the proof of your note on United Europe.

Here are some comments:

1. At present there is only one plan under discussion for a European army.

2. This is the so-called Pleven Plan. This has made technical progress, but it is in political trouble over fundamental questions of sovereignty. This plan does not permit national armies to exist in participating countries, except for overseas garrisons. Its purpose, at least in French and Italian minds, is to pave the way for federation. I have never thought it possible that we could join such an army.

3. The late Government made clear its attitude to the army, and to the Schuman Plan, in a joint statement by the Foreign Secretaries of France, the United States and the United Kingdom, at Washington in September. I quoted this in the House in my speech in the foreign affairs debate, and it was generally approved. Schuman was also fully satisfied with it as a statement of our position, when I discussed it with him in Paris before the debate.

4. Now that the Pleven Plan is running into trouble in the countries that put it forward, we are being made the whipping boy.

5. That appears to be Strasbourg's only activity at this time.

6. It is possible that the Pleven Plan will fail, though it has the backing of General Eisenhower. If so, we shall be back again with the problem of Germany's part in Western defence.

7. Opposition to a German national army is strong, not only in France; Adenauer has never advocated it.

8. Even more important is the reaction of Russia, who would view the creation of a German national army and her admission to N.A.T.O. which must follow, as a major threat.

Conclusion:

(a) We should support the Pleven Plan, though we cannot be members of it. This is what the Americans are doing, and it is the course Eisenhower wants us to take.

(b) If the Pleven Plan does collapse, we should try to work out a more modest scheme with our allies, based upon the technical military arrangements agreed upon, but without elaborate political superstructure.

(c) Any move for (b) will require careful timing. If we move too soon, the Pleven Plan will collapse, and we shall be told we have killed it.

Letter from Eden to Churchill, 1 December 1951, from Anthony Eden, *Full Circle*, London, 1960, pp. 33–4.

2.14 Policy agreed

Though they did not see eye to eye over the European army proposal, Churchill did not resist the policy which Eden advocated. Following talks with the French government at the end of 1951, both Prime Minister and Foreign Secretary agreed upon a policy of British association with an eventual EDC. This was put to Cabinet by Eden and given approval. It spelled out a formula which he was to follow towards all supranational organisations which emerged on the Continent and foreshadowed the solution which he was to arrive at when the EDC finally collapsed in the summer of 1954.

I ask for authority from my colleagues to make an approach on these lines at an appropriate moment to the French Government, if the results of the present six-Power meeting in Paris warrant it.

1. To associate themselves with any suitable machinery that may be set in order to supervise the general political common interests of the EDC and the United Kingdom in means of European defence;

2. To associate themselves with any suitable machinery that may be set up for permanent consultation between the United Kingdom Chiefs of Staff and the equivalent military authorities on the EDC;

3. To undertake that the United Kingdom forces on the Continent shall, subject only to the requirements of SACEUR,[6] operate as closely as possible with the [EDC] forces, and shall be tied up with them as far as possible in matters of training, administration, supply, etc.;

4. To accept at once individuals, units or formations, of the EDC for training with British formations in Germany and elsewhere and, in addition, to lend British officers and unite, where this is administratively possible, to EDC formations. This might well be easier to develop in the Air Force than in the Army; for example it may well be practicable to integrate European Air Force Wings into British tactical Air Force groups: we should be ready to examine this possibility;

5. To declare that in war SACEUR has authority to allot British formations as he thinks best in the light of this military situation at the time; this authority includes that of placing British formations under command of a EDC Commander if convenient. To declare further that in peace we would make British

[6] Supreme Allied Commander in Europe.

formations temporarily available for training with European Defence Forces under the overall command of SACEUR;

6. To declare that it is the intention of the United Kingdom to maintain armed forces on the Continent for such time as she deemed necessary having regard to the requirements of the European Defence Community and the United Kingdom's special responsibilities in Germany.

Public Record Office, London, CAB 129/48, C(51)62, memorandum by Eden, 29 December 1951.

2.15   British 'association' with the EDC spelled out further

> Clearly, Eden would have preferred Britain's 'association' with the EDC to have remained as loose as possible. What faced him, however, were French, and also Dutch, fears of a militarily revived Germany, which were used to try to lever Britain into full participation in the EDC as a counter-balance to the Germans. These attempts were firmly resisted. But this pressure, plus insistence from Washington that Britain do more to help get the EDC Treaty signed by the Six, led to a series of concessions by Eden, culminating in early 1952 in the offer of an Anglo-EDC Treaty by which Britain would provide automatic support for the EDC if it was attacked. This, along with American pressure in Paris, helped get the EDC Treaty signed on 27 May. The Anglo-EDC treaty was signed on the same day.

Proposed Tripartite Declaration

On February 14th the Cabinet approved in principle a suggestion that Her Majesty's Government might make a declaration of support for the European Defence Community (EDC) and I later informed my colleagues that a draft had been prepared during the meeting of Foreign Ministers held in London on February 17th – 19th. The draft of this declaration, which will be tripartite, is still being discussed with the United States and French Governments. The idea is that the United Kingdom and United States Governments should mark their interest in the EDC by declaring their intention to maintain armed forces in Europe and to take a hand through the North Atlantic Treaty Organisation if any member of the Community threatens to break away.

Proposed British Guarantee

It was also suggested that Her Majesty's Government should make a separate declaration on their own, and a text was in fact agreed in Lisbon between M. Schuman and myself. We are now, however, being pressed to go further than this. We have been warned by the French Ministers that, before the final debate in the French Assembly, we shall once more be strongly pressed to join the EDC. This I have declined to do. In the meantime we have been asked to enter into a Treaty relationship with the EDC by extending to Germany, Italy and the European Defence Forces the undertakings we have given to France, Belgium, Luxembourg and the Netherlands, under the Brussels Treaty, to afford automatic military assistance if they are attacked. In return we should receive from the Community reciprocal undertakings....

Recommendations

My recent conversations in Paris have left me with the clear impression that the EDC is not likely to be established unless we respond to this latest proposal....

Mr Schuman did not dispute my conclusion that any undertaking on our part must be limited to the period during which the United Kingdom is a party to the North Atlantic Treaty. He even said that a British declaration in place of a treaty would be sufficient. But it seems to me that if we are willing to enter into this commitment it should be given a formal document, and this applies equally to the reciprocal commitment from the EDC upon which we must of course insist. I propose therefore that these commitments should be embodied in an appropriate treaty instrument concluded between the EDC and the United Kingdom.

... When making this communication I would propose to repeat with all possible emphasis that this is the limit to which the United Kingdom can go in the way of association with the EDC; that we cannot accept membership and that we shall be unable to respond to any future pleas that we must take yet further steps and actually join the EDC in order to save the whole project from failure.

Public Record Office, London, CAB 129/50, C(52)92, memorandum by Eden, 28 March 1952.

2.16 'All was signed and sealed, but far from delivered'[7]

> The EDC Treaty had now to be ratified by the participating governments. It was expected that this would be done within a matter of months. This proved to be wildly optimistic. Especially exasperating for the British was the French insistence on further guarantees against German militarism before the Treaty could be ratified. This, it was noted, was likely to have dismal repercussions on relations between France and Germany – the two principals in the integration process.

When the three Western Foreign Ministers met Dr Adenauer in London nine months ago, Dr Adenauer told M. Schuman with some truth that the Germans were apt to be an arrogant people and that their arrogance was being fed by the spectacle of French terror of Germany. The Germans, he said, had taken a frightful beating during the war and were amazed to find that fifty million victorious Frenchmen were shaking in their shoes in front of fifty million defeated, disarmed, and dispirited Germans. It was all very bad for the Germans.

I recall this incident because I am beginning to notice in Germany a growing, quite good natured contempt for the French; the sort of contempt which hearty sixteen-year-old boys have for timorous old ladies.

Even in Hitler's early days of power the German General Staff had respect for the French Army and this in turn led to some brake being put on German plans and aspirations. I know we can do nothing to instil any courage or confidence into the French, but unless they can be a little more robust in their conduct of affairs they will soon create a situation in which Germany will regard them with complete contempt and cease to pay the slightest attention to anything they may say. This state of affairs will not conduce to French security.

[7] Eden, *Full Circle*, p. 47.

Others were more sympathetic to the French plight and noted that the difficult, six-year-old struggle between France and the Communist-led Vietminh in Indo-China had begun to magnify French fears over the rearming of Germany.

Politically Indo-China is now in the heart of Europe. None of the major problems which beset Europe can be solved in isolation from what happens in South-East Asia. French doubts about the ratification of the Treaty of the European Defence Community stem largely ... from their fear that the drain of Indo-China will prevent them from providing forces equivalent in strength to the German forces, and as long as these doubts persist the problems of Europe will never be settled.

Public Record Office, London, CAB 129/56, C(52)375, Sir Ivone Kirkpatrick, British High Commissioner in Germany, to Eden, circulated to Cabinet, 30 October 1952; FO 371 101060/130, Oliver Harvey to Eden, 19 November 1952.

2.17   Pressure from Washington

Pressure to move closer to the EDC in order to help secure ratification came not just from the French but also from Eisenhower, the new American President, who used his wartime friendship with Churchill to urge the Prime Minister to make one of his 'great and "booming" speeches in its support'.[8]

Dear Winston,

... There is another subject of vital interest to us both and concerning which I have spoken to you a number of times. It is the need, in Europe, for uniform progress on the Common Defense Plan and for greater political and economic unity. In recent weeks I have been consulting with official and unofficial representatives from some of the countries in Western Europe.

---

[8] Public Record Office, London, PREM 11/1074, Roger Makins, British ambassador in Washington to Churchill, 21 June 1953.

Almost without exception, they have said that a more emphatic *public* endorsement by Great Britain of these projects would be helpful, particularly in securing the support of most of the Socialist Party in France, which is more or less the key to that country's probable action. Permit me to say again that I should very much like to see you seize some appropriate opportunity to make a major address on the general subject of greater European military and economic unity, stating in your own inimitable and eloquent way the things that *you have already announced that Britain is ready to do* in support of these purposes. Such might just happen to be the decisive influence.

As ever,

Ike.

Public Record Office, London, PREM 11/1074, Eisenhower to Churchill, 7 April 1953.

2.18   More pressure from Washington

> In June Churchill was temporarily disabled by a stroke and there was no 'booming' speech in favour of the EDC. Eisenhower gave dark warnings of the effect that the failure of the EDC might have on American opinion and policy towards Europe.

Dear Winston,

I shall, of course, keep completely secret the character of your illness. I am cheered to note that you are very hopeful, but of course I agree that your doctors must make the final judgement on the question of your return to full duty. My prayers are with you ... I note with interest your thought about a four-power meeting and French action on the EDC. If the French Parliament should reject it, I cannot possibly over-emphasize the adverse effect such action would have on public opinion in this country. Our people and our good results. They believe earnestly that only closer union among the nations of Western Europe, including Western Germany, can produce a political, economic and military climate in which the common security can be assured. Personally,

I think our people are right on this point – but the important fact is that they most earnestly believe they are right. As a consequence if they find their judgments and convictions completely ignored by the principal NATO country in Western Europe, it will indeed take genuine efforts to keep our people from washing their hands of the whole affair. To my mind that kind of a result would be catastrophic for us all....

Not for one moment do I believe that I am overstating the adverse results in this country that would follow failure of the EDC to achieve French and other Western European endorsement. On the contrary, we are already suffering because of dilatory tactics heretofore pursued in the region. Soon we are to present to the Congress a request for appropriation to support the Mutual Security arrangements in Western Europe, and we are going to have a lot of trouble with those who believe that Europe has no intention of unifying or of adopting EDC.

I have sent messages both to Holland and Belgium urging early ratification so as to bring additional pressure on France. I have done this not because I want to interfere in anybody else's business, but because I know what it means in this country. This also is the reason why I continue to ask every personal and official friend that I think I have in Europe to get in and help. Possible alternatives to NATO's and EDC's success are too alarming to contemplate. If this country should return, no matter how reluctantly, to a policy of almost complete isolationism, or at the very least, to a 'Western hemisphere only' philosophy of security and interest, then Heaven help us all....

As ever,

Ike.

Public Record Office, London, PREM 11/1074, Eisenhower to Churchill, 6 July 1953.

2.19 High temperatures at Bermuda

Churchill's illness had forced the postponement in June of a conference at Bermuda between the heads of government of Britain, France and the United States to discuss West European security. His remarkable recovery allowed it to take place on 4–7 December. The conference was used by the British and Americans in an unavailing attempt to push the French into ratification. The French wanted more concessions from the British. The outcome, as Eden's Private Secretary records, was annoyance and frustration all round.

Eight solid hours. Winston made another long speech on security assurances, starting with the statement that he had been 'looking round for something to please the Russians' and by the time we came to the communiqué the atmosphere was again very unsatisfactory. Trouble started at once when the French refused a reference to 'European unity'. When I remember how we clung to the word 'unity' to placate the French who were pressing upon us 'European union' I realize how far we have come downhill in the last two years. Outbursts by Eisenhower and Winston, former left the conference table in a rage, came back, having changed for dinner, sat another four hours. I heard him say to Dulles,[9] 'Never again will I come to one of these, unless it is all prepared and agreed beforehand.' Winston said: 'The EDC is dead. We want a German army.' Bidault[10] tried every means to get us to say in the communiqué that ratification of EDC depends on problems still to be discussed with the allies, i.e. to put the blame on us. We refused. Everybody very angry, appeals, sentiment, Bidault looks like a dying man, Laniel[11] is actually dying upstairs. At 1 a.m. a formula was found which Bidault agreed to try and sell to Laniel. He sent it up. Nothing happened for half an hour. Finally A.[nthony]E.[den] suggested going himself to plead with Laniel. I went up with him to the bedroom where the Prime Minister of France, totally inexperienced in foreign affairs and new to office, was holding up the entire proceedings hour by hour. The French advisers all in despair: '*Nous ne pouvons plus rien.*' A.E. succeeded in his mission and came down with the text agreed. Everyone worn out and bad-tempered. Later the PM visited A.E.'s bedroom in a single vest, having walked all down the passage looking far from decent.

[9] John Foster Dulles, United States Secretary of State.
[10] Georges Bidault, French Foreign Minister.
[11] Joseph Laniel, French Prime Minister.

Evelyn Shuckburgh, *Descent to Suez: Diaries 1951–56*, London, 1986, p. 116, diary entry 7 December 1953.

2.20 Churchill's reaction to American pressure

When combined Anglo-American attempts at Bermuda to cajole the French to ratify the Treaty failed, John Foster Dulles, with less finesse than his President, reverted to the theme that the United States might wash its hands of Europe. He spoke publicly of a possible 'agonising reappraisal' of American policy. Churchill initially thought the warning 'salutory'[12] and seemed, at Bermuda, as this excerpt from the diary of Lord Moran[13] suggests, to have accepted the consequences of American threats with equanimity.

The P.M. is surprisingly well after yesterday's performance.

P.M.: 'The communiqué was a flop. In refusing EDC the French may have thrown away the last chance of saving France.'

Moran: 'The Americans will take it badly?'

P.M.: 'Oh very badly. They may pull out, and if they do we shall follow.'

Moran: 'What will happen then?'

P.M.: 'Oh, France may become a kind of Czecho-Slovakia, a satellite of Russia.'

Moran: 'And where does Adenauer come in?'

P.M.: 'The Germans would form a secret army, but the Russians will attack them before they can do anything. But my view is that the Russians are afraid. They may listen to reason.'

Moran: 'What kind of defence could we put up if things go like that?'

P.M.: (*shrugging his shoulders*): 'What the Americans call peripheral defence: Iceland, Spain, Turkey, wherever there are bases. Bidault is prepared to sacrifice his career for EDC. He knows it is necessary.

Lord Moran, *Winston Churchill: The Struggle for Survival 1940–65*, London, 1968, pp. 509–10, diary entry 8 December 1953.

[12] Public Record Office, London, PREM 11/1074, Churchill to Eisenhower, 19 December 1953.

[13] Lord Moran, Churchill's doctor and confidant.

63

2.21   Eden's response to American pressure

Eden was less composed than Churchill and viewed an
American withdrawal from Europe as much a threat to
British interests as to the French. He wanted the EDC to
materialise and was prepared to contemplate even further
concessions – short of joining – to get it.

You will have seen the records of our talks in Bermuda about the
EDC.

I think that we have got to think seriously what we can do to
save the whole plan which at present seems very shaky. I think
that quite a large part of the French difficulty in Bermuda was
due to the impending Presidential elections which caused both
Laniel and Bidault to take up extreme positions and that when
these are over we may hope to see the French Government, if it is
reformed on the right lines, get down once again to the task of
securing ratification. But they will undoubtedly have great
difficulty and, considering the importance of the issues at stake,
we must really search our minds as to whether there is not
something we can do to clinch the matter at the time of the
crucial debates in the French Parliament. As you know, the whole
future of American support for Europe may turn on this.

I would therefore like you to look once again with the utmost
seriousness at the possibility of some new form of help by us to
the EDC project. I do not believe that any of the ideas for
guaranteeing to keep our troops on the Continent for a pro-
longed period or promising not to withdraw forces without
effective EDC consultation are on the right lines. For one thing,
we could not do anything of that kind unless the Americans did
so too and although this is what the French are now aiming at,
no doubt in order to help us, I see little prospect of that. Rather I
feel that we should look again at our own association with the
EDC itself. The idea I have in mind will no doubt seem startling
to you and may be impracticable. It is that we might offer to
form some special UK unit, no doubt recruited on a voluntary
basis, which we could put into the EDC. I see of course grave
practical difficulties on this but the idea might perhaps be
connected up with that of ensuring our continued and very vital
requirement of German support units by turning the German

Service Organisation into an EDC unit. The troops, if they were to be on a level with EDC forces, would no longer be UK troops and would be part of the international force for all purposes. Strictly speaking, they could not be withdrawn by us, though I dare say we could make some arrangement for replacing regiments and individuals. I do not want to make more detailed suggestions because I am sure the right thing would be for you to look into it with a fresh mind and see what can be worked out. The main point I want to make is that I am convinced we are moving towards a real turning point in the whole relationship of the US to Europe and that we must have recourse to all our imagination and ingenuity to help the EDC through. It is, of course, essential to keep anything of this kind up our sleeve until the psychological moment after the French Presidential elections. No word should get out now that we are even considering alternative arrangements.

> Churchill, perhaps persuaded by Eden, eventually came to grasp the dangers of an American fall back to what was now being called 'peripheral defence'.

We are actively supporting the Americans over EDC. If it fails or evaporates in indefinite delays, a great effort must be made to achieve the same results (i.e. German Rearmament) through a recasting of NATO. The danger which I fear the most is Mr. Dulles' 'agonised reappraisal'. Peripheral defence may well be doom-laden. Its possibility has not receded....

Public Record Office, London, FO 800/778, Eden papers EU/53/ 47, Eden to Lord Alexander, Minister of Defence, 12 December 1953; CAB 129/70, C(54)271, note by Churchill, 18 August 1954.

2.22 'A miserable contemptible Government'

> Eden's objective continued to be that of nudging the French towards ratification while, at the same time, considering contingency plans in case this failed to occur. The former

remained the priority and in April 1954 Bidault was offered an Anglo-EDC Treaty as a further inducement. However, the French remained, as Evelyn Shuckburgh's account reveals, a source of intense exasperation to the British.

> Then came messages from Paris that the French do not want us to announce our new measures of association with EDC as planned on 5 April. A.[nthony]E.[den], furious, kept saying they are such a miserable contemptible Government they cannot even say 'yes' when we offer them help. He was minded to reject their request, and publish on 5 April, but we shall have to stop him doing that. Selwyn [Lloyd] and Tony [Nutting] agree; the whole point of our measure is to help, not embarrass the French. A.E. said, 'Evelyn, put it in your diary; never in all my experience have I known such conduct.' But poor Bidault is doing his best; he wants to get his Parliament into recess before he signs the agreement with us. A.E. should understand that – and will.

Shuckburgh, *Descent to Suez*, pp. 156–7, diary entry 31 March 1954.

2.23   The end of the EDC

> Three and a half years of persuasion, concessions and veiled threats had failed to dissipate French fears of an armed Germany or their reluctance to hand over control of the French army to a European authority. On 30 August 1954, the National Assembly threw out the EDC Treaty. This was not entirely surprising. Nor was the invective which now poured upon France. Churchill, it seems, had conveniently forgotten his own part in inspiring a European army.

When, about four o'clock, Winston woke from an hour's sleep he could not stop yawning.

'The world,' he began, 'is in a terrible condition. The throwing out of EDC is a great score for the Russians.'

Then, waking up, his voice rose:

'The French have behaved in an unspeakable way, execrable. No thought at all for others, ingratitude, conceit,' he spat them out with intense distaste. 'I cannot feel the same about them in the future.'

I asked him if he had been surprised by the majority[14] in the French Chamber against EDC.

'No,' he answered, 'Mendès-France[15] said there was no chance of getting it through.' Then, with more animation: 'But look at the swine, wasting three vital years. It was their own invention. They made us do it. My very pleasant relations with Anthony make things more difficult. I would have liked to control this business, but if I did I would be taking the bread out of Anthony's mouth after denying him the square meal he so much wanted.' He grinned broadly....

Moran, *Winston Churchill*, pp. 595–6, diary entry 2 September 1954.

2.24 Eden's triumph

Churchill's irritation was mirrored in Washington and Bonn. Plans for further European integration seemed to have collapsed. German rearmament was no further forward and, without this, an American contribution to the defence of Western Europe was in doubt. In short, the Western Alliance was in disarray. Eden now managed to produce an alternative to the EDC which restored German self-esteem, calmed French fears, retained the American commitment to Europe – and all without loss of British sovereignty to a supranational body. The trick was to expand the 1948 Brussels Treaty to include Germany (and Italy). This would allow controlled German rearmament as a prelude to eventual membership of NATO. Agreement was reached at an international conference in London in September and the restructured Brussels Treaty was termed the Western European Union (WEU). As a further palliative to France, a British promise to keep forces on the Continent so long as its alliance partners desired was held in reserve. This concession was produced during the London conference.

The object of the meeting was to discuss the proposal that the Foreign Secretary should, at a crucial stage of the Nine-Power

[14] 319 to 264 with abstentions.
[15] French Prime Minister 1954–55.

talks at present taking place, be empowered to give an undertaking –

> (i) that the UK would station on the Continent the effective
> strength of the British Forces now assigned to SACEUR,
> i.e. four divisions, and the Tactical Air Force or whatever
> [was] regarded as their equivalent fighting capacity;
>
> (ii) not to withdraw the forces against the wishes of the
> majority of the Brussels Treaty Powers who should take
> their decision in knowledge of SACEUR's views.

This undertaking would be subject to revision in the event of an
overseas emergency or of the maintenance of such forces in
Europe imposing too heavy a drain on the external finances of the
UK. In the latter event HMG [Her Majesty's government] would
be able to ask that the financial conditions should be reviewed by
the NATO Council.

THE FOREIGN SECRETARY said that while such an offer
would not be justified merely in order to satisfy the French
Assembly, all the other powers assembled in London felt that a
British offer of this kind might save the situation....

It was agreed that, while the Prime Minister might telegraph to
President Eisenhower with the object of encouraging a cor-
responding move on the part of the US Government, there would
be no advantage in making a British offer conditional on the
American decision since if America withdrew from Europe the
whole NATO defence system would in any case collapse.

In these circumstances it was generally agreed that the Foreign
Secretary should have the right to offer, at the time he thought
appropriate, the stationing in Europe of four divisions of the
British Army, or their equivalent in fighting strength, as well as
the Tactical Air Force.

Public Record Office, London, CAB 129/71, C(54)302, summary
of a discussion at 10 Downing Street, 28 September 1954.

2.25   Eden's motives

NATO had been saved, but the EDC had been lost. Was this
Eden's intention all along? Variations on the WEU had been
under discussion in Whitehall since 1951. But this was not

deviousness. They had been shelved for fear of Britain being sucked into the EDC and from an unwillingness to be accused of sabotage. This extract from a note to Churchill in the summer of 1953 suggests that Eden was genuine in his hope that the EDC would materialise and that it was the 'best bet' as a solution to the intricate problem of German rearmament.

1. Atlantic Pact and work of last two years is beginning to produce results.

2. Though Western Alliance creaks, its defensive power in Europe is growing. EDC is signed; Russians don't want to see it in force.

3. A German contribution to western defence is indispensable; Germany should carry the burden of such a contribution. EDC is best instrument available to give it effect.

4. There are signs that the Russians' hand is being more intelligently played. e.g. Austria.[16]

5. Immediate aims of Soviets is to disrupt western alliance. They are making some progress towards it.

6. Americans are at present more friendly to British than British to Americans. This more friendly attitude may not last and I am not sure that we deserve that it should.

7. The smaller, poorer and more experienced partner is easily resentful. We have to be aware of encouraging anti-American prejudice. 'We will go it alone' cries can be dangerous in either country.

8. No sufficient evidence yet to determine cause or consequence of Beria's[17] fall.

9. If Foreign Secretary's meeting does take place there is no reason why agenda should not in practice be widened if desired. But if this meeting or any other is to be successful we must know our German policy in advance and have discussed and agreed it with our friends.

10. To press for early operation of EDC still seems our best bet. I am not convinced we couldn't get it. But this would mean some

---

[16] The Soviets were taking a softer line on the post-war occupation of Austria.

[17] Head of the Soviet secret police, arrested and executed after Stalin's death in 1953.

plain and private speech to the French by Britain and the United States.

Public Record Office, London, PREM 11/426, Eden to Churchill, 3 August 1953.

2.26   Eden and the ECSC

Eden followed a similarly benign policy towards the Coal and Steel Community. An Anglo-ECSC Treaty was signed in December 1954. This may be seen as a parallel to the Anglo-EDC Treaty offered in the spring. Both had something to do with an attempt to fulfil the promise to associate Britain with moves towards integration. The Anglo-ECSC Treaty sprang from what were called the Eden Proposals of early 1952. These, as we see here, were an attempt to demonstrate a more positive policy towards Europe and to inject new vitality into the Council of Europe by merging the organs of that body with those of the nascent ECSC and EDC.

I have been giving some thought to the difficult problems relating to the Council of Europe. Here are some reflections.

The movement for unity in Europe, which led to the creation of the Council of Europe, is now flowing along two main streams: the Atlantic Community, a wide association of states which, without formal surrender of sovereignty, is achieving increasing unity of purpose and action through the machinery of the North Atlantic Treaty Organisation: the European Community, a small group of states which are moving towards political federation by the progressive establishment of organisations exercising supra-national powers in limited fields.

The Council of Europe is stranded between these two streams. Many members of the Assembly feel despondent about the future of Strasbourg and some are prepared to admit that, in its present form, the Council of Europe is out-of-date and superfluous. In an attempt to acquire 'limited authority but real powers', the Assembly has produced a draft new statute of the Council of Europe, which will be on the agenda at the next session of the Committee of Ministers. This transforms what is now a purely consultative body into a quasi-federal institution with legislative and executive powers and the right to be consulted by member Governments on certain matters within its competence. It would therefore be difficult for us to remain in the Council of Europe if the new statute were adopted.

A more promising future for the Council of Europe would lie in a remodelling of the organisation so that its organs could serve as the institutions of the Schuman Plan, the European Defence Community and any future organisations of the same structure and membership. The advantages would be:

(a) The Council of Europe would be given valuable work to do;

(b) the reduplication of European bodies would be avoided;

(c) the Schuman Plan and the European Defence Community would be provided with ready-made machinery....

Memorandum by Eden, 15 February 1952, *DBPO: Series II, Volume I* , pp. 826–7.

2.27 Eden's reputation defended

> Eden's approach to co-operative developments in Europe was not that of a visionary, but nor was it anti-European. It was founded on the premises that Britain was still a significant military power, was still an important figure on the world stage, and was an industrial and trading power greater than any of its European neighbours. It was identical to the policy pursued by Bevin in the last years of his life and differed little from the self-styled 'pro-Europeans' in his own party. The following assessment by a man who worked closely with Eden during these years seems an appropriate judgement.

The accusation that he personally stifled the pro-European inclinations of the Churchill administration of 1951 rankled with him to the end of his life. In April/May 1969 he wrote me three letters on the subject and sent me a copy of a five-page memorandum which he had prepared refuting suggestions to this effect by Mr Macmillan, Lord Boothby and others. The very last time I saw him before his death he asked me whether I could not find, amongst my papers or my memories, material for proving the contrary.

People who had committed themselves to federalism and European union and found that their own Conservative Government was no more prepared to support such things than the Labour Government had been, naturally liked to attribute this to the short-sightedness or folly of individual colleagues rather than to the mood of the country. My reply to Eden's question in 1969 was that I did not think he should worry so much about his record on this point; he had, in my opinion, been correct in his judgement as to how far the British could be persuaded to go towards integration in Europe. In my last letter to him, of 12 May 1969, I said, 'It still seems to me quite clear that the British were not ready to put their forces into anything like the EDC in 1951.'

I think subsequent experience has endorsed this. The agreements of 1954, which brought the Federal Republic of Germany into NATO and into the Western European Union, and which included undertakings by the United States and the United Kingdom to keep forces on the Continent, were more realistic and have been the main foundation of European security for the last thirty years. They were to a great extent Eden's creation and they should be sufficient to protect his memory against the vain imaginings of Lord Boothby.

Shuckburgh, *Descent to Suez*, pp. 17–19.

3

Going it alone 1954–58

The creation of the WEU out of the fiasco of the EDC was not only a personal triumph for Anthony Eden, it also seemed to demonstrate the shortcomings of federalism and the wisdom of the British approach to European co-operation, that is, the loose inter-governmental path rather than the tight supranational way. This turned out to be an enormous misjudgement, and in June 1955, the six ECSC states met at Messina in Sicily to consider ways of strengthening and deepening the ties between each other. The British were invited to the post-Messina discussions, but their participation was tentative. Buoyed up by their apparently successful stance over the EDC, the British saw no convincing reasons to alter their position. Over two-thirds of British trade was still outside Europe, and especially with the Commonwealth. By this time, however, it was beginning to be recognised that Western Europe was an increasingly important market for British manufactures. This meant that there was now a feeling that Britain could no longer afford to look as benignly upon further consolidation between the Six as it had during the Schuman Plan period, the more so as it soon became clear that the Six were indeed moving towards the formation of a customs union which would eventually provide a single external tariff for its members. This time their objectives had to be either confined or foiled. The chosen instrument for this was a proposal for the FTA, which would ease commerce between the competing states without the application of any external tariff, leaving Britain's preferential trade with the Commonwealth unharmed. The FTA was thus founded on mixed motives. As an institution distinct from but associated with that which the Six proposed, it was expected to provide an attractive alternative to a customs union. At times, however, it took on the appearance of a spoiling tactic. The strategy failed and by the end of 1958 the Treaty of Rome, signed and ratified by the Six, inaugurated the European Economic Community (EEC), with Britain on the outside.

3.1 France behind the times

The British stance on integration was often reinforced, as this comment from a leading figure in the Foreign Office indicates, by a view that France, judged to be the hotbed of European federalism, was in a state of apparently irreversible decline.

I believe that for the last 50 years or so France has stood still in almost every field of human endeavour. When I was a boy France was in the van in the development of the motor car and the aeroplane. In the world of medicine and physics France occupied a leading place. French literature and French theatre were vital. The French school of military thought was recognised even by the Germans to be first-class for reasons into which I need not enter now. But today one has the impression that France is unable and unwilling to move with the times. They know that air power is important, but they cannot build an air force; they know that armoured divisions are essential, but they cannot equip them with tanks. In electronics, atomic energy, and indeed in every field of scientific endeavour, the French are hopelessly behind. Politically they are also living in a bygone age.... Most Frenchmen fear the Germans more than they fear the Russians....

If all this is true, and I believe it to be true, it seems to me that with the passage of time France will be more and more left behind; and a consciousness of her inadequacy will increase French defeatism and the present French reluctance to embark on any positive policy....

Broadly speaking I think we shall have to recognise that ... France is necessary to us for geographical and other reasons, and that we shall have to make the best of a bad job. But it is always dangerous to cherish illusions, and any belief that France is likely to become a good job is, I think, an illusion.

Public Record Office, London, FO 371, 112778, Sir Ivone Kirkpatrick, Permanent Under-Secretary at the Foreign Office, 30 April 1954.

3.2   Britain on the sidelines

> Despite the ignominious collapse of the EDC proposal, the six member states of the ECSC met at Messina in June 1955 to discuss the possibility of extending their co-operation. Though their objectives were unclear, the outcome proved, in the long run, to be momentous. The principal decision was to set up a committee chaired by the Belgian federalist Paul-Henri Spaak. The British were invited to join this committee. They decide to do so in order to avoid the criticism of being 'anti-European', but cautiously on the fringes and with the intention of guiding the discussion along lines amenable to themselves.

The *Chancellor of the Exchequer* [R. A. Butler] said that at Messina the six ECSC countries had resolved to make further advances towards the economic unification of Europe, and to invite the United Kingdom Government to take part in the work of a Preparatory Committee. Some of the specific objectives of the six Powers ... for example, the creation of a common organisation for the peaceful development of atomic energy and the establishment of a common market in Europe, seemed likely to involve duplication with other arrangements or were fraught with special difficulties. He therefore recommended that we should agree to take part in the work of the Preparatory Committee as observers only and subject to suitable reservations about our attitude to the specified objectives.

In discussion support was expressed for the view that the utmost caution was required on our part in relation to the specified objectives of the six ECSC countries. It was suggested, on the other hand, that we ought not to create the impression that we disapproved of their efforts to promote a greater measure of economic integration between themselves.

The Foreign Secretary [Harold Macmillan] said that, while we should preserve our full freedom of action and make it clear that we were not in any way committed to joining any body or bodies which might eventually be set up, we might be able to exercise a greater influence in the forthcoming discussions if we were to enter them on the same footing as other countries concerned and not in the capacity of an observer....

Public Record Office, London, CAB 128/29, CM(55)19, minutes of Cabinet meeting held on 30 June 1955.

3.3   The British in a bind

> The term 'observer' was favoured by the Treasury, but 'delegate' was preferred by the Foreign Office. In the end, it was decide to compromise and send a British 'representative' to the Spaak Committee. Having decided to participate, however, the British found themselves in a quandary. Their very presence could be taken to mean agreement to decisions which they found objectionable. But withdrawal would court disruption, for which they might well be blamed for, as the British representative noted, some of the Six still seemed to be waiting for a British lead.

At this stage, I think, we, as United Kingdom representatives, may be confronted by something of a dilemma. If we take an active part in trying to guide the final propositions into a form which is acceptable to us, it will be difficult to avoid later on the presumption that we are, in some sense, committed to the result; it might, for instance, be said that if the United Kingdom had not insisted upon such and such a point, the conclusions of the report would have been different and that, therefore, the United Kingdom must be held responsible for its actions in such a case. On the other hand, if we sit back and say nothing, it is pretty certain that many more things will get into the report which would be unpleasant from the British point of view whether we in the end took part in the Common Market or not....

Clappier, who is acting rather intermittently as the chief French representative on the Common Market Committee, asked me to have tea with him yesterday and spoke very frankly about the French attitude. He said bluntly that, as far as he could see, France would be willing to go quite a long way and quite quickly, in the direction of the Common Market, but on one condition only, namely that the United Kingdom was also taking part, or in some way closely associated with the operation. On the other hand, he thought that if the United Kingdom seemed to dissociate herself from what was going on, France would make no move whatever. I replied that this, though not very surprising, was obviously very embarrassing to us. I thought personally that HMG would be most unlikely to give any clear undertaking to participate in a Common Market, but on the other hand we should not want to slam any doors and it was, therefore, clearly important from the French point of view that the report which emerges from here should not have such form or content as would make it necessary for us to say we could have nothing to do with it....

Public Record Office, London, T232/431, Russell Bretherton, British representative on the Spaak Committee, to the Treasury, 4 August 1955.

3.4   Impatience with the Spaak Committee

By November, four months after it had been set up, the British began to distance themselves from the Spaak Committee. They had not been able to guide the discussions along lines acceptable to Britain, partly, it was felt, because the French had their own particular agenda. However, the French seemed unlikely to be able to carry the Americans or the whole of the Messina group along with them. Some distraction was now sought and the wider, non-supranational, OEEC[1] was chosen by the British to perform this task.

Taking into account also the Common Market question ... we feel that Messina is a doubtful, if not actually wrong, approach and that the OEEC is a better one. We are not ashamed of our own 'European' record, whether in the military or economic sphere, and we hope not to be blamed for supporting OEEC as

---

[1] Organisation for European Economic Co-operation. Set up in 1948 to co-ordinate Marshall Aid, it developed a wider brief of easing trade restrictions between the West European states. It had no supranational or federalist objectives.

the proper economic vehicle for the 'European Idea', even if it does suit us to do so. This is not to say we are against special groupings of OEEC member countries for functional purposes such as nuclear energy. But we should be much happier if these could be organised from within the OEEC and we shall remain a bit sceptical and suspicious of the Monnets of the European world who, having failed so far in their special political objectives, are now using the slogan of 'economic integration' as their stalking horse.

What in any case are they likely to achieve? No doubt the French would be glad to export their economic shortcomings, and see that much attraction in a Common Market. But, if they succeeded, the result would be a discriminatory bloc most unwelcome to us, to say nothing of the Americans and all the non-Messina members of the OEEC. If they fail, as seems more likely, we shall have had another futile exercise, comparable to the EDC but even worse, in one way, to the extent that it would have damaged if not destroyed the OEEC. The Germans for their part are obviously not in the least keen, apart from Adenauer, on this whole business of economic integration; and who would carry out the process, for it would take many years to put theory into practice, after he had passed from the scene.

In the OEEC, on the other hand, we can provide a loose enough framework not to irk the Germans (or tax the French) unduly. We have the Americans here. And we can play our role, without getting into conflict with our own wider interests....

We realise there is an outside chance that the Messina politicians may yet succeed in squaring the economic circle either for nuclear energy or for the wider question of a Common Market, and in case they do we shall be duly cautious in our dealings with the Six. But meanwhile our hopes are with the OEEC and such schemes as can be devised with their agreement in that forum. Apart from nuclear energy ... we do not exclude the possibility at a future point of some further general economic initiative in OEEC. But don't bank on this!

Public Record Office, London, FO 371, 16054, Sir Ivone Kirkpatrick, Permanent Under-Secretary at the Foreign Office, to Sir Gladwyn Jebb, British ambassador in Paris, 25 November 1955.

3.5 France and the Spaak Committee

The British were not entirely wrong to be sceptical about the outcome of the Spaak Committee. Robert Marjolin, a French official who was then Secretary-General of the OEEC, provides us with a picture of French hostility to the Committee's idea of a common market.

It was in the spring of 1956 that France's reactions to the Spaak Committee made themselves known, that French officialdom and the leading representatives of industry and agriculture expressed their fears, their hostility towards the common market project. Up to that point no one had thought that a venture of this kind could even take shape on paper, let alone become fact. And suddenly here was a text which, of course, had not been formally accepted by anyone, but whose provisions to a large extent prefigured a possible European customs union. Above all, it became known that certain members of the government, and important ones at that – President of the Council Guy Mollet, Foreign Affairs Minister Christian Pineau – were favourably disposed. There was a small group of 'Europeans', namely Jean Monnet, myself and a few others who were determined that Europe should get over the EDC failure. But the obstacles were enormous. Almost all of them were manifestations of the fear that had seized French business and especially government officialdom at the idea that the wall of protection, of all kinds, built up during the prewar, war and postwar years might one day come down and that French industry would then have to face foreign competition without customs duties, quotas or state subsidies. The very thought made the interested parties feel as helpless as Spartan babes on the mountainside.

Robert Marjolin, *Architect of European Unity: Memoirs 1911–1986*, London, 1989, pp. 284–5.

3.6 Sabotage?

In fact, British interest in the OEEC had declined since the winding up of the Marshall Plan three years earlier. But it was, at this stage, the only alternative they had to try to wean the Messina powers away from a customs union. It was expected that both the Americans and the Germans would be allies in this. Each was, for different reasons, supposedly cool towards Messina. This seriously miscalculated both the strength of German support for co-operation and the increasing determination of the United States to back Germany within an integrated Europe as a bulwark against the East. Worse than this, Britain's formal withdrawal from the Spaak Committee, when it came on 7 December, beat the publication of the Committee's final report to the gun and was issued, not to the Six, but to the Council of the OEEC. To Spaak and to his colleague Johan Beyen, the Dutch Foreign Minister, it all looked suspiciously like an attempt at sabotage. Their blistering response came, symbolically perhaps, at the next meeting of the Council of the British-sponsored WEU.

Following from Secretary of State [Harold Macmillan]

The Chairman [M. Beyen] sprang on us a new agenda on which the first item was economic cooperation in Europe.

M. *Spaak* led off by saying he had been concerned for some time over the future of the WEU, and this concern had been greatly increased by the recent British *démarche* in the OEEC, and various capitals. Her Majesty's Government had adopted an unfavourable, even hostile, attitude towards the plans of the Messina Powers as being contrary to the true interests of Europe and had indicated their opposition to those plans. Whilst the Messina Powers had never expected the United Kingdom to participate fully in their plans, he was surprised that the United Kingdom should now oppose the idea of a common market and he thought it particularly unfortunate that this opposition should be expressed in another international organisation. If the members of WEU ventilated their differences before others, he took a gloomy view of the future of WEU. He thought it would have been proper and desirable that the members of WEU should first discuss their attitude towards European economic co-operation in their own Council.

M. *Beyen* said he had been greatly surprised by the British *démarche* in which the United Kingdom had indicated that they felt compelled to inform the Messina Powers that they could not participate in the common market for three reasons: first, because of their links with the Commonwealth; second, because a common market could not be reconciled with a one world system; third, because a common market would impede the workings of the OEEC. He did not wish to go into the substance of these issues but only to discuss the significance of the step taken by the United Kingdom. The Messina Powers had not asked for the views of Her Majesty's Government; the present British initiative had been spontaneous. Did it mean more than it actually said? If the British *démarche* became known to the public it would be interpreted as a British condemnation of the Messina plans. This would be serious because the Six considered their plans important, not only for their economic content, but also for their political significance as a means of binding the European countries closer together. He concluded by asking me the direct question, whether our declaration meant more than it said and whether in fact it constituted condemnation of the Messina plans.

I pointed out that I had had no prior warning that this subject would be discussed and I was therefore not in a position to make a considered statement. I assured M. Spaak that he was wrong in thinking that we wished in any way to injure WEU.... Our declaration was not condemnation of the six-Power plans but it was a warning that we must not divide Europe in the course of trying to unite it....

M. *Spaak* then reaffirmed his criticism of our action in bringing this question before the OEEC.... His impression was that the British statement in the OEEC had gone further than I suggested. It had been not merely a proposal for a study but had been, in fact, a declaration against a common market. He went on to say that the six countries could not pursue simultaneously two policies, one on six-Power basis and the other in OEEC. They would have to choose....

Public Record Office, London, FO 371, 116057, Macmillan's report of the meeting of the WEU Council, 14 December 1955.

3.7 British apprehensions

Spaak's and Beyen's complaints were not entirely without foundation. In contrast to the discussions of the Schuman

Plan five years earlier, the British were tempted to follow a line of, as they called it, 'insuring against the success' of the common market. A spluttering concern is also now discernible in London that the Six might just bring it off. These worries were to continue. Added to them were Cold War considerations. West Germany was being rearmed, the USSR had formed the Warsaw Pact in May 1955, and had recognised East Germany as a sovereign state in September. But now that 'economic integration' had been pulled further out of the bag at Messina, it could not easily be put back. Though it might be a development uncongenial to Britain, it was beginning to be recognised that something was needed to strengthen the bond between the Western European states – if only to control a resuscitated Germany.

THE CASE FOR A CLOSER LINK WITH EUROPE

This review stems from the growing fear of a course of events in Europe which would disrupt our interests and undermine our security and economy.

This threat arises from the growing strength and independence of Germany, coupled with the growing deterioration of France. Germany can no longer be forced to remain within the orbit of the West; and might well see advantage in neutralism and fishing in troubled waters. Without Germany the future of the Alliance on the Continent would be precarious.

We must thus consider how Germany might be brought to see her interest in remaining allied with the West. This would almost inevitably involve a closer association of the United Kingdom with the Continent; a closely-knit Western Europe, militarily and economically strong, would otherwise pass under German hegemony, and might well become as dangerous to our interests (though in a different way) as a disrupted Europe.

There are thus two threats – one that Germany will dissociate herself from the West, and the other that Germany, while remaining with the West, will establish a domination over Europe. This illustrates the dilemma for the United Kingdom which is presented by the Messina schemes. If a proposal for a common market of the 'Six' came into being, it might help to tie Germany into the West, but it would be so dangerous to our

economic interests that we should have to make special arrangements with it, even at the expense of our interests elsewhere. If,
on the other hand, it did not come into being this would mark
one more failure of the European countries to work together –
and a highly publicised one – and one more step towards the
disruption of Europe, unless something new could be found to
replace it.

If it were possible for the United Kingdom to develop a closer
economic association with Europe, without weakening our links
with the Commonwealth and the United States, this would be a
powerful reinforcement for the West. Our weight would balance
Germany's and the closer link between our world-wide
associations and the Continent of Europe would extend the
opportunities to be derived from the association – and thus the
attractions in it and the likelihood of success in the main object.

Public Record Office, London, FO 371, 122075, report of a working group of officials from the Foreign Office, Treasury, Board of
Trade and Commonwealth Relations Office, 20 April 1956.

3.8   Home truths to the Americans

It was important to the British to try to convince the
Americans that what the Messina states had in mind should
be resisted. The two being as one on this crucial issue
would be a clear reinforcement of the 'special relationship'.
There was also a firm belief, put forward here by the
President of the Board of Trade, that a protectionist trading
group in Europe could only be damaging to the United
States and to Anglo-American relations. Again, at the core
of this concern, were apprehensions over Germany.

I am convinced that the Americans are in a fool's paradise about
Messina, and I strongly recommend that you [Eden, then Prime
Minister] and the Foreign Secretary [Selwyn Lloyd] should seek to
bring home to President Eisenhower the gravity of the dangerous
situation which is rapidly developing against the interests of both
our countries and all our joint work since the war to build up a
'one world' trading system.

The Americans think in terms of customs unions, and the idea of a customs union in Europe has a strong appeal for them. But this is all an illusion. A customs union of the scope and scale envisaged by the Messina countries whatever their good faith, would take a generation or more to achieve. The practical result for years to come would be that these countries would attenuate tariffs and other trade obstacles piecemeal between themselves and discriminate against the rest of us. No fine words would disguise the reality of a discriminatory block, in the heart of industrial Europe, promoting its own internal trade at the expense of trade with other countries in the free world.

I do not see how any British government could afford, in the face of this, to go on with existing Anglo-American policies of non-discriminatory, multilateral trade.... Certainly the Conservative Party would not stand for it. Our businessmen would be ousted from the European markets through discrimination in favour of their German competitors. They would look to us to fight their case – to break the discrimination or to discriminate back....

How all this would end up I cannot pretend to foresee. The whole basis of the post-war settlement of our international trade relations would be in the melting pot. No doubt we would find a new pragmatic basis to arrange our affairs – we have the economic power to negotiate and we would use it. But it would put a desperately severe strain on our relations with the Americans. For they, whatever the rest of us might or might not gain, would be bound to lose across the board – and their immediate reaction would be to put the blame on us. However difficult it may therefore be to persuade the Americans, I think it is vital that you should give a plain and unmistakable warning to President Eisenhower.

Public Record Office, London, FO 371, 122022/11, Peter Thorneycroft, President of the Board of Trade, to Eden before a visit by the Prime Minister to Washington, 20 January 1956.

3.9 Plan G

Possible responses to the Messina powers' common market had been investigated in Whitehall as the Spaak Committee deliberated. Six variants, in the shape of Plans A to F, were put forward. By September these had crystallised into an agreed option, Plan G, which was put to the Cabinet by Macmillan on 14 September, at the height of the Suez Canal crisis.

SUMMARY OF PLAN G

Description of the Plan

The United Kingdom should enter a partial free trade area with the Customs Union of the Messina Six (Benelux, France, Germany, Italy) and all other OEEC countries that wished to join (probably Norway, Sweden, Denmark, Switzerland, Austria).

The area would probably not include either our own dependent territories or those of the European countries; this must remain undecided, however, until we know the Europeans' view about this; our own Colonial territories are being consulted about their possible interest.

The free trade area will cover all commodities, *without exception* except foodstuffs.... The exclusion of foodstuffs is an essential condition on which we should insist without qualification, both in the interests of home agricultural policy and in the interests of the Commonwealth.

Within the free trade area, tariffs, protective quotas and other protective devices would be reduced and ultimately abolished in defined and timed stages over a period of about a decade.

We should retain our existing freedom of action in our tariffs on imports from the rest of the world ...; this is the essential difference between a free trade area and a Customs Union. There would be no change in our present obligations regarding fee entry of Commonwealth goods, and of course we should be under no commitment to discriminate in Europe's favour against the Commonwealth.

We should insist that there should be no discrimination by the Messina Six in each others' favour and against us. This implies the same time-table for tariff reduction throughout the whole free trade area.

Public Record Office, London, CAB 129/83, CP(56)208.

3.10 A shift in policy

The advantages of the FTA over a Messina-type common market would, for Britain, be threefold. There would be no external tariff. It would be an entirely industrial system, with agricultural products excluded. In this way Commonwealth preferences would be unaffected. Political sovereignty would not be an issue as there would be no reference to federalism. It was not intended to be a wrecking scheme or an alternative to the Six's customs union, which was now, more or less, accepted as likely to happen. It was an attempt to supplement and to maintain British control over events which were now taking place. There was also the possibility that the FTA would have beneficial effects on the British economy. As Anthony Eden implied in Cabinet, the FTA represented a new direction in British policy.

The Prime Minister, summing up the discussion, said that we were confronted with a dilemma. An economic plan based on the Commonwealth connection would no doubt have been preferable and the Secretary of State for Scotland [James Stuart] had expressed to him misgivings about the risks to the Conservative Party in appearing to abandon traditional policies based on maintaining the solidarity of the English-speaking peoples in favour of closer union with European nations. But there was little prospect of devising a policy based on the Commonwealth connection: the Australians appeared to be determined in their pursuit of their present commercial objectives and both Australia and New Zealand were bound to be attracted, if only for reasons of defence, towards an increasingly close association with the United States. The attitude of the Asian members of the Commonwealth towards the British connection was uncertain and they diverged from us on many matters. Unless, therefore, we were capable, acting alone, of meeting formidable European competition in overseas markets, there seemed no alternative but to base our policy on the proposed plan for closer association with Europe, or some suitable variant or extension of it.

Public Record Office, London, CAB 128/30, CM(56)66, 18 September 1956.

3.11   The lessons of Suez

The Messina initiative clearly raised questions about Britain's position in the world. The Suez crisis magnified these. The Egyptian nationalisation of the Suez Canal in the summer of 1956 preoccupied the British until the ignominious cease-fire of Anglo-French invading forces in November. The British felt let down by the Americans, who refused to give crucial financial support as the crisis peaked. The French were embittered against the British, who left them in the lurch 23 miles down the Suez Canal. Among a number of the lessons of Suez for Anthony Eden, as he noted twelve days before his resignation as Prime Minister, was one concerning Britain's relations with Europe. It was a lesson, like some of the others, only imperfectly learned.

The Prime Minister has written the enclosed 'thoughts' on the general position after Suez. He would like the Foreign Secretary [Selwyn Lloyd] to see them, on a personal basis, and would no doubt be glad to have any comments on them from him....

We have to try to assess the lessons of Suez.

The first is that if we are to play an independent part in the world, even on a more modest scale than we have done heretofore, we must ensure our financial and economic independence. Since we have no raw materials but coal, this means we must excel in technical knowledge. This in its turn affects our military plans....

In the strategic sphere we have to do some re-thinking about our areas of influence and on the military bases on which they must rest. Some of the latter seem of doubtful value in the light of our Suez experience....

One of the lessons of Suez is that we need a smaller force that is more mobile and more modern in its equipment....

At home the events of these months must create some deflation, though probably in geographically limited areas, e.g. the motor car industry in the West Midlands. This again may not be entirely unhealthy and if and when the oil begins to flow again the economy may be healthier as a result. The most anxious fact on the home front is I think the alarming increase in the cost of the welfare state. Some of this, e.g. education, is a necessary part of our effort to maintain a leading position in new industrial developments....

The conclusion of all this is surely that we must review our world position and our domestic capacity more searchingly in the light of the Suez experience, which has not so much changed our fortunes as revealed realities. While the consequences of this may be to determine us to work more closely with Europe, carrying with us, we hope, our closest friends in the Commonwealth in such development, here too we must be under no illusion. Europe will not welcome us simply because at the moment it may appear to suit us to look at them. The timing and the conviction of our approach may be decisive in their influence on those with whom we plan to work.

Public Record Office, London, PREM 11/1138, note by Eden, 28 December 1956.

3.12   Suez and the integration of Europe

Anthony Nutting, who had special responsibility for European matters in the Eden government and who resigned over British policy during the Suez crisis, later recalled that Suez demonstrated Europe's weakness and accelerated the process of integration.

I think as far as the French were concerned [Suez] had a very considerable influence. The French, of course, were furious with the Americans, so equally were we. But it made the French all the more convinced that they must go as fast as they could towards European integration because they could not, as they saw it, rely on the United States any longer. Then, course, when the whole thing collapsed, and we and the French fell out indeed, they felt let down by Britain as well. So in that sense I think it undoubtedly helped to speed up the pace of European integration.

To a certain degree the British were pushed in this direction too. In October 1956, when Suez was approaching its climax, Macmillan publicly announced the FTA proposal. In late November, as the crisis fizzled out, he revealed details to the House of Commons. Suspicions still remained, however, that Britain's intention was to wreck the common market. This apprehension also helped push the

Messina powers forward. Uncertainty over British objectives was picked up by the Swiss press.

All newspapers see a connection between the Suez Crisis and the United Kingdom's change of attitude but consider the prime motive was the fear of being left at the starting post by the Common Market scheme. Some conclude that if the latter were now abandoned the UK would drop the Free Trade Area scheme. One paper goes so far as to say that the UK move may be nothing more than an ingenious delaying operation.

Anthony Nutting in Michael Charlton, *The Price of Victory*, London, 1983, p. 220; Public Record Office, London, FO 371, 122035/279, British embassy in Berne to the Foreign Office, 17 October 1956.

3.13   British apprehensions increased

The Treaty of Rome, which prepared the way for the EEC and for co-operation in the peaceful uses of atomic energy (Euratom), was signed by the Messina powers on 25 March 1957. This gathering momentum among the Six increased British apprehensions but did not dislodge them from their position that the FTA was the best way forward. The Treaty had yet to be ratified by the separate governments, which might still be persuaded against. To the usual arguments, Macmillan, who had succeeded Eden as Prime Minister in January, gave characteristic emphasis to Cold War considerations.

The Chancellor of the Exchequer [Peter Thorneycroft] said that there was a considerable body of opinion in Europe which wished to see the European Customs Union established without a Free Trade Area. The negotiations about the latter were proceeding very slowly, mainly by reason of the dilatory attitude of the French Government. If, however, the Customs Union came into being unaccompanied by a Free Trade Area, the United Kingdom would be confronted with a European economic *bloc* which would discriminate against our exports and we should be liable to

89

suffer severe damage as a result both of the loss of European markets and of the intensified competition from members of the Customs Union in markets overseas....

In discussion there was general agreement that the Treaty of Rome derived basically from political considerations and that its real objective was the creation of an integrated European Community, capable of exerting a considerable political influence in its own right.... If this effort to establish a European 'third force' succeeded in its present form without our being associated in some positive fashion with the new alignment of power in Europe, the consequences would be very grave. Our existing European policy would be undermined and our special relationship with the United States would be endangered if the United States believed that our influence was less than the European Community.

In these circumstances it was necessary to consider urgently what measures could be taken to persuade the Members of the Customs Union that an industrial Free Trade Area would be the natural complement to their own policies and that they would be ill-advised to confine their efforts to creating the Customs Union in a context which excluded the participation of the United Kingdom....

The Prime Minister summing up the discussion said that the situation which had developed was serious.... [Failure to obtain the FTA] must lead inevitably to the disintegration of the European policy which, in common with our allies, we had hitherto pursued, involving the collapse of the North Atlantic Treaty Organisation and the existing system of defence against the Soviet Union. It was therefore in the interests of all Western European Governments that the conception of the Customs Union should be extended to include an industrial Free Trade Area within which the United Kingdom could maintain and strengthen its association with Western Europe. But if the members of the Customs Union felt unable to cooperate effectively with us to this end, they must expect us to adopt such measures of self-protection as we could devise in terms of our commercial policies.

Public Record Office, London, CAB 128/31, CC(57)37, 2 May 1957.

3.14 'A whispering campaign is going round Western Europe'

At the same time, European suspicions of British motives had deepened, and there was some desperation to eradicate these as a prelude to selling Britain's policy.

A whispering campaign is going around Western Europe to the effect that we are trying to sabotage the ratification of the Treaty of Rome.... The American Ambassadors in the capitals of the Rome Treaty countries were reporting freely to Washington that the British Government was set on 'bringing down the Rome Treaty'....

It seems to me that this misconception of our policy could be very dangerous.... The resentment would jeopardise the chances of getting the Free Trade Area concept successfully launched. Yet the true position surely is that we do *not* want to sabotage the ratification of the Treaty of Rome – or still less to have it thought in Europe that this is what we are trying to do. What we want is for the Treaty to be ratified but to be supplemented by the association of ourselves and other countries in the Free Trade Area. The problem is to get that position understood.... I wonder whether we ought not to think of a major speech by the Prime Minister in which he would endeavour to put our whole policy in its true perspective.

Public Record Office, London, BT11/5553, Sir Frank Lee, Permanent Under-Secretary at the Board of Trade, to Sir David Eccles, President of the Board of Trade, 26 April 1957.

3.15 Selwyn Lloyd's 'grand design'

As it turned out, British policy over the next few months served to reinforce the concerns of the Europeans. In April 1957 the Foreign Secretary, Selwyn Lloyd, announced his so-called 'grand design' to rationalise the representative bodies of the Council of Europe, the WEU and the ECSC into a single, purely consultative, assembly. British assertions that all it was trying to do was to bring a sense of order and purpose to the activities of the various European organisations failed to quell suspicions that it was aimed to dilute the objectives of the Six.

When I dined with the German Counsellor on Friday he expressed misgivings about current feelings in Bonn. In particular he thought that there were some who thought the Grand Design just a clever plan for wrecking the intimate association of the Six. Apparently the Germans are holding a Conference of Ambassadors in Berlin at the moment in which their representatives at the capitals of the Six were giving vent to suspicions of this country. For these reasons Herr von Braun believes that your visit to Bonn will be very important and that you should concentrate on European problems.

Public Record Office, London, PREM 11/1841, Philip de Zulueta, Macmillan's Private Secretary, to Macmillan, 28 April 1957.

3.16 'A dose of humility is recommended'

Ironically, the grand design was intended, in part at least, to deflect criticism from the British decision to reduce its forces in Germany – only three years after the commitments made at the time of the founding of the WEU. The reduction was part of a defence review by the Minister of Defence, Duncan Sandys, which, in the aftermath of the Suez crisis, had opted for reliance on Britain's nuclear capacity. Both initiatives were the focus of intense hostility on the Continent, where they were perceived as further demonstrations of Britain's limited interest in Europe. At home, the pro-European *Economist* noted that they had 'revealed a powerful undercurrent of suspicion of British motives' and that 'a dose of humility is recommended'.

The British Government's efforts to make co-operation with Europe a main pillar of its policy has been through a black fortnight. The Council of Europe received the British 'Grand Design' for a new western assembly with a barrage of devastating criticism.... In the North Atlantic Council at Bonn, Mr. Selwyn Lloyd's exposition of Britain's new defence philosophy of relying on the nuclear deterrent was received with indignant European criticism, and he was forced to mince if not eat his words.... Suspicion that Britain's new smiles towards Europe are just another trick in the old national game of perfidious Albion has come to a head....

Their doubts have been inflamed by the new British defence policy. Whatever its wisdom, the new policy has been introduced in a way that offends the spirit of the European alliance. The decision to concentrate on nuclear weapons was made without regard to NATO's own struggles to find a common solution to the military, economic and political problems of tactical nuclear warfare. The decision to cut the Rhine army was, even more, a plain retreat from obligations....

In the differences over the free trade area the Government has had worse luck than it might have hoped. The scheme is, after all, a revolution in British policy and the greatest single demonstration of the sincerity of Britain's new interest in Europe. Yet even here British attitudes – an air of generosity, a sense that the decision to interest ourselves in Europe is a gift from an insular St. Nicholas to the continental children – arouse resentment....

It is a broader conflict of interests, however, between the common market countries and Britain that has bogged down the free trade area negotiations.... After their long months of negotiations, the six common market governments, above all that of the French, are anxious to get their treaty ratified without further delay. The British government, on the other hand, sincerely wishing to develop the free trade area around the common market, would like the treaty to be modified in certain ways.... British requests for alterations look much like 'sabotage'. They are not; some modifications in the common market treaty will probably have to be made. The problem is to make them quickly enough (so that the two schemes can have a chance of coming into operation together) without holding up the ratification of the Rome treaties which have already been signed.

'Albion in the dock', *The Economist*, 11 May 1957.

3.17 Attempting to square the circle

These were perceptive comments. The British were trying to have it both ways. If the FTA came off, they would be able to sell their manufactured goods in Europe without impediment from the external tariff of the Six. At the same time, they, though not the Six, would be able to buy cheap food and raw materials from the Commonwealth. But, as *The Economist* also pointed out, inadequate though it might be, the FTA did represent a tilt in British thinking towards a fumbling recognition that close British col- laboration with the Western European states had a virtue in itself. Indeed, the publicised version of Selwyn Lloyd's 'grand design' was the pale shadow of an attempt to revive something like the 'third force' idea, but this had been severely mauled by the Cabinet in January. In May 1957 Lloyd was still tempted to view this as an alternative to a common market.

I have been considering what further initiatives it is possible for us to take with regard to Europe.

(a) *Economic.* I am afraid we have to wait and see how the ratification of the Rome Treaties proceed. Any step taken by us pending those ratifications would be suspect. All we should do on the economic side, I think, is to make our own plans in case the common market is not ratified, and in the meantime trying to prevent countries like Denmark going into the common market because such adhesions would make the free trade area all the more difficult.

(b) *Political.* The more we push the European Assembly a la 'grand design', again the more suspicious will the other Europeans be.... Even if we were to accept the subsidiary ideas of joining up OEEC and the Council of Europe, or putting in WEU with the common market and the Euratom assemblies, I think at this moment we should do more harm than good for the same reason. Of course, if we were to offer to set up a WEU Council of Ministers with some powers as a council that might be regarded as coming further into Europe. As previously indicated, the difficulty is what powers you could transfer to a WEU Council of Ministers.

(c) *Military.* The above considerations bring me to the con- clusion that the most useful ground for advance is in the military field at the moment. One thing would be an offer of the bomb to WEU. Another thing would be the offer of our tactical atomic stockpile. A third would be to press on rather more sensationally with the idea of a common research and development programme and common production programmes. Under this third heading, the Ministry of Defence have, I know, always been of the opinion that there is not much which actually can be done owing to our tie-up with the United States over almost every type of weapon.

I still think that there is something in the ideas in the Cabinet Paper [of 5 January 1957] which I produced, i.e. that in the long term the sound thing is to try to make Western Europe the third nuclear military power. Many of our then colleagues however expressed strong disagreement with that idea because of its effect on our relations with the United States.

Public Record Office, London, PREM 11/1841, Selwyn Lloyd to Macmillan, 28 May 1957.

3.18   The uncertain progress of the Treaty of Rome

The possibility, expressed by Selwyn Lloyd, that the Treaty of Rome might not be ratified by national parliaments existed until the end of 1957. France presented the most uncertainty and there was a real possibility that French demands would destroy the proposed common market as they had the EDC. Robert Marjolin, the chief French negotiator of the Treaty and a firm supporter of European co-operation, faced serious opposition from those who, like the former Premier, Pierre Mendès-France, feared for French interests.

Fallacies die hard, especially when they are presented under a veneer of good sense. For an example I need look no further than the speech made by Pierre Mendès-France in the National Assembly on January 18, 1957 in the course of a preliminary debate on the Common Market when the drafting of the Treaty of Rome, in its essentials, was almost complete. This exceptionally intelligent man, who was so often right, but was often wrong too, was singularly misguided in the attitude he took that day with regard to the ongoing negotiations, one which he was to confirm six months later by voting *against* the Treaty's ratification.

Freedom of movement for manpower was the first to come under attack, Pierre Mendès-France fearing that the Italians would export their unemployment. At that time, of course, Italy was suffering from large-scale unemployment and under-employment. In the event of an economic crisis, he maintained, emigration of Italian workers to France would be compounded by that of the German unemployed, who were traditionally more mobile than their French counterparts. On the other hand, in periods of buoyant economic activity, we would have to contend with formidable competition in the Common Market. Certain of our industries might be unable to adjust or would adjust badly. The result would be unemployment in various sectors of our underdeveloped regions. The populations of those regions might then be driven to emigrate, or else have to accept a very low standard of living *in situ*. Attracted by higher living standards, the Italians would flock into France and, in certain circumstances at any rate, the French into the Ruhr. An apocalyptic vision.

Marjolin, *Architect of European Unity*, pp. 289–90.

3.19   Searching for the initiative

Though the FTA was judged to have the virtue of helping to develop the efficiency of the British economy by opening it up to competition, it was also felt that this was as far as Britain could go in devising a European economic bloc. To go further would not only risk domestic dissension, but also damage Commonwealth and American connections. There was also the worry expressed most consistently, but not solely, by Macmillan, Prime Minister since January 1957, that a high-tariff common market would divide Europe between those who were in it and those who felt unable to join. Advantage would go either to the Soviets or to Germany. On the other hand, it was proving impossible to dispel the view on the Continent that, as one British official put it, the FTA was 'tailor-made for us'. In the frustrating search for some political angle which would meet the ideas of the federalists and win over the Six, Macmillan demonstrated some inclination to return to sabotage.

I have been thinking over the useful meeting we had last Thursday, and I understand that you are having a further meeting about this subject this afternoon. As I said at that meeting, I feel sure that the pressure for European integration, though expressed in economic terms, really derives from the strong desire of many European countries for some form of closer *political* association. We should take advantage of this, since while we are in something of a strait jacket as regards economic integration, we may well be able to show Europe that we are prepared for a closer political association. The following points ought to be considered urgently:

1) ... We might agree that the management of a European Free Trade Area should be left to a European managing board. This might well be called a 'supra-national' institution. But does it matter?

2) We cannot afford to wait till November. Some earlier initiative, on a high level and with political connotation, seems to be necessary.

3) For this purpose, it might be necessary to entrust our interests in this matter to a special Minister, who would co-ordinate the activities of and be helped by all the Departments concerned (principally the Treasury, Foreign Office and the Board of Trade).

4) We must not be bullied by the activities of the Six. We could, if we were driven to it, fight their movement if it were to take the form of anything that was prejudicial to our interests. Economically, with the Commonwealth and other friends, including the Scandinavians, we would stand aside from a narrow Common Market. We also have some politico-military weapons.

What the above amounts to is this: that we must take positive action in this field, to ensure that the wider Free Trade Area is more attractive than the narrower Common Market of the Six. We must take the lead, either in widening their project, or, if they will not co-operate with us, in opposing it.

Public Record Office, London, PREM11/2133, Macmillan to Thorneycroft, President of the Board of Trade, 15 July 1957.

3.20 An apostolic mission

The 'special Minister' suggested by Macmillan turned out to be Reginald Maudling, Paymaster General, to whom

Macmillan gave the 'apostolic' task of holding the eleven states interested in the FTA together while links were attempted to be forged with those who had now signed the Treaty of Rome. It was an unenviable task. The negotiations of the Maudling Committee, which lasted from October 1957 until their collapse in November 1958, were characterised by certain peripheral concessions by Britain, as Macmillan had earlier hinted there might be, towards supranational management of the FTA, but none whatsoever on fundamentals such as the inclusion of foodstuffs in the FTA or over the necessary harmonisation of trade between two groupings which would have different tariff structures. The fact was that the FTA did not offer much to the Little Europe of the Six other than the fear that it would, intentionally or otherwise, swamp them. Macmillan's response to these frustrations became increasingly hysterical.

I think sometimes our difficulties with our friends abroad result from our natural good manners and reticence. We are apt not to press our points too strongly in the early stages of a negotiation, and then when a crisis arises and we have to take a definite position we are accused of perfidy. I feel we ought to make it quite clear to our European friends that if Little Europe is formed without a parallel development of a Free Trade Area we shall have to reconsider the whole of our political and economic attitude towards Europe. I doubt if we could remain in NATO. We should certainly put on highly protective tariffs and quotas to counteract what Little Europe was doing to us. In other words, we should not allow ourselves to be destroyed little by little. We should fight back with every weapon in our armoury. We should take our troops out of Europe. We would withdraw from NATO. We would adopt a policy of isolationism. We should surround ourselves with rockets and we would say to the Germans, the French and all the rest of them: 'Look after yourselves with your own forces. Look after yourselves when the Russians overrun your countries.'

Public Record Office, London, T234/203, Macmillan to Selwyn Lloyd, 24 June 1958.

3.21 Fortress Britain

This sort of division was, of course, what the FTA had been devised to prevent. Matters deteriorated when Charles de Gaulle returned to power in France in the summer of 1958 and began successfully to court the German Chancellor, Adenauer. The Germans remained a constant source of apprehension to the British because of Germany's potential for dominating the common market. Yet, up to now, there had remained a hope that they would find it impossible to work with the French. This was fast disappearing.

I would be grateful if you and the Chancellor of the Exchequer could consider what we are to do if the negotiations for the European Free Trade Area break down completely and the Treaty of Rome Powers begin to operate a system clearly hostile to our commercial interests. What remedies have we? Can we take action on the economic plane, in GATT [General Agreement on Tariffs and Trade] by a tariff war, or by some other forms of discrimination to counter their discrimination against us?

By political action. I hardly think we could justify remaining in NATO and keeping four divisions of our troops at considerable expense to defend militarily a group of countries who were carrying on an economic war against us. Finally, I would like to consider how far this should be made clear to the French and the Germans. I have already said something pretty stiff to de Gaulle but then he will have forgotten it by now. I said the same to Adenauer the other day. He was shocked but impressed. We may be accused of the usual perfidy if we do not make it clear while there is still time how serious we would consider a breakdown and how it would cause us to review all our commitments. Fortress Britain might be our right reply.

Public Record Office, London, T234/378, Macmillan to Derek Heathcoat-Amory (Chancellor of the Exchequer) and Selwyn Lloyd (Foreign Secretary), 15 October 1958.

3.22 'The crowning folly of the twentieth century'

The expectation had been that de Gaulle's nationalism would make him something of an ally with the British in curtailing the impact of the common market. This over-looked the General's determination to hem in the Germans and his pragmatism in recognising that France had negoti-ated significant concessions within the Six. By November he had also obtained agreement on unanimity towards the FTA from the other five, as well as support for the French position from the United States. All this, plus a new air of decisiveness in Paris now that de Gaulle was in charge, presented a gloomy prospect for the British.

RECORD OF A MEETING HELD AT 10 DOWNING STREET ON THURSDAY, NOVEMBER 6, 1958

The Foreign Secretary [Selwyn Lloyd] said that he and M. Couve de Murville [French Foreign Minister] had just finished a bad meeting at which they had finally torpedoed the Free Trade Area. Mr. Maudling had left the meeting very depressed. In particular the morning talks had revealed a difference to the approach to the problem which had not previously been apparent. It seemed as if the French Government's position now was that they could not contemplate any arrangement which did not allow the Six to have a special position between themselves.

M. *Couve de Murville* said that he would not take quite as pessimistic a view as the Foreign Secretary. At the same time it was true that the French Government could not contemplate the régime inside the Six being exactly the same as that inside the whole Seventeen [members of the OEEC]; the common market must not completely disappear. The reason for this was that France had taken on many commitments in the common market and could not afford to take on the further commitments which a Free Trade zone would impose.

The Prime Minister said that he was very sorry to hear this. It seemed to him that no serious progress had been made in the last year and the French Government's policy was constantly chang-ing. The meetings in November would settle the Free Trade Area finally one way or another. When M. Couve de Murville demurred the Prime Minister said that he could not see how, if things were not settled at least in principle by January 1 [the date when the European Economic Community of the Six was to be formally set up], there was any hope of progress for the future.

Once the two communities in Europe started to go their separate ways, it would be almost impossible to bring them back again....

M. *Couve de Murville* said that unfortunately the question of agreement in principle for a Free Trade zone was so closely linked with the detailed conditions necessary for any such zone that the French Government were unable to express agreement in principle until the details had been worked out.

The Prime Minister said that in that case he was very pessimistic. It depressed him to feel that the French Government had decided that Sparta and Athens must quarrel. The Russians were getting stronger all the time and here was the free world voluntarily weakening and dividing itself. History would regard this as a tragic decision and the crowning folly of the twentieth century in Europe.

The Foreign Secretary said that of course the political consequences of failure to have a Free Trade zone would be very great; they would perhaps extend to the Western European Union and to NATO.

Public Record Office, London, FO 371/13451.

3.23 Pointless threats

Macmillan was clearly concerned with the peril, as he saw it, of weakening Western Europe by dividing it into potentially competing economic blocs. It was also a desperate posture in a deteriorating bargaining position. However, as was pointed out in the Foreign Office, it was unlikely to have much influence on de Gaulle.

The crisis which has arisen as the result of its becoming apparent that the French are not going to agree to the kind of Free Trade Area which we have contemplated has many features in common with the crisis which arose in 1954 when the National Assembly refused to vote for the ratification of the EDC Treaty. What was then at stake was the defence of Europe. Unless the Germans could be armed there were not enough men to man the line. Today the issue once again is the defence of Europe, or at least that is what we say. If Europe is going to be divided economically

101

it will end in its also being divided politically, this will split the Alliance, we shall be increasingly unable or reluctant to station troops on the Continent, etc. etc. But it was no use in 1954 propagandising the French Deputies about the consequences for the defence of Europe of a refusal on their part to ratify the Treaty. It was like water off a duck's back. So today I very much doubt whether any amount of gloomy prognostication about the effect on the defence of Europe of a breakdown in the Free Trade Area negotiations will by itself have very much effect on General de Gaulle. In his message of last July the Prime Minister told the General that the effect of a breakdown would be 'tragic' but this message does not seem to have disturbed him very much. Another point of similarity between the present crisis and the 1954 crisis lies in the degree of disappointment and fury aroused in London by the final realisation that the project in question is not going to go through. In the case of the EDC Treaty it was obvious for months before the debate in the Assembly that it was going to be rejected; and yet all the plans made in the FO [Foreign Office] were based on the supposition that it would be accepted and those concerned with the business refused until the very last moment to believe the evidence of their eyes. There is a further point of similarity. The opponents of the EDC Treaty in France were quite unmoved by the argument that they had the rest of Europe against them. They did not mind this a bit and indeed some of them were rather pleased about it. The opponents of the Free Trade Area are also unlikely to be moved by this argument.

Public Record Office, London, FO 371, 134505, Sir Arthur Rumbold, Assistant Under-Secretary at the Foreign Office, 7 November 1958.

3.24 The FTA torpedoed

On 14 November the French gave the death blow to the Maudling Committee by insisting that there could be no FTA without a common external tariff. A lingering hope remained that France's common market partners, especially the Germans, might resist de Gaulle's veto, but this soon proved illusory. To the irritation of the British, Adenauer had already been wooed by de Gaulle during two personal meetings in September and November. By the end of 1958 Britain faced the prospect of isolation from the EEC, which would come into operation on 1 January 1959, with no realistic alternative in view.

It is clear that General de Gaulle has really quite dismissed the idea of a Free Trade Area and the only consolation, if it can be called that, is that he is also apparently anxious to play down the Common Market as something of no political importance.

The prospects for the Free Trade Area certainly look very bad. In France no one seems to be in favour of it, and ... it seems clear that Dr. Adenauer is only in favour of the Free Trade Area if it does not disrupt the Common Market. The dilemma seems to be that Dr. Adenauer would, if necessary, sacrifice the Free Trade Area to the Common Market whereas General de Gaulle at least would rather wreck the Common Market than accept the Free Trade Area. In the absence of any effective pressures by us which could be exercised on both the French and the Germans, I cannot help feeling that the Free Trade Area is now finished.

In the economic field we do not seem to have any effective cards to play and the only pressures we could bring would therefore be political. Here I suppose that our main card is NATO and our contributions to the defence of Europe, particularly Germany. If, however, we try to use threats of withdrawal from Germany and perhaps of an independent policy about such questions as Berlin, we should certainly alarm the Germans, but probably not the French. If we alarm the Germans sufficiently we might, perhaps, cause them to put pressure on the French that the Common Market would collapse or be very much watered down, but we are unlikely to be able to get the Free Trade Area. But if Dr. Adenauer had to choose between seeing our troops (but not the Americans) leave Europe and the break up of the Common Market, I do not know which he would choose.

My own conclusions are therefore that our only course is *either* to try to break up the Common Market *or* to concentrate on watering it down and securing the best possible terms. The first course would probably involve stimulating anti-German feeling in France, and the second course may involve forming a grouping of the non-Six; both are disagreeable and would have bad political consequences, but short of a change of heart by the French, there seems little else to do.

Public Record Office, London, PREM 11/2826, note to Macmillan from his Private Secretary, Sir Philip de Zulueta, 30 December 1958.

4
The turn towards Europe 1959–61

The Macmillan government had no contingency plan for the failure of the FTA proposal. But in the spring of 1959 negotiations were opened between the seven non-EEC states which had been involved in the FTA discussions, with the objective of constructing a smaller free trade area. By the end of the year the product of these talks, the Stockholm Convention, brought Austria, Britain, Denmark, Norway, Portugal, Sweden and Switzerland together in EFTA. The ease with which EFTA was created is partly explained by the momentum generated by the earlier FTA discussions and by the fact that the new grouping exhibited no pretensions towards a federal Europe.

Though the British might argue that EFTA would offer them considerable trade benefits, this was really whistling to keep up spirits, and even before the Stockholm Convention was signed, it was being recognised that to pursue EFTA was to follow the wrong trail. The President of the Board of Trade summed up the feelings of many of his colleagues when he admitted that anything other than a free trade area in association with the EEC would be 'a climb down – the engineer's daughter when the general manager's has said no'.[1] The reality was that EFTA was born of resentment at de Gaulle's imperious scotching of the FTA project and a desire to prevent non-EEC states from drifting into the orbit of the Six. While it allowed that 'the Seven is not a despicable grouping in economic terms,' a Cabinet Committee also conceded that EFTA had been 'brought together by "ties of common funk" rather than by any deeper purpose or by geographical contiguity.'[2]

---

[1] Public Record Office, London, T 234/377, Eccles to Macmillan, 14 July 1958.
[2] Public Record Office, London, CAB 134/1820, report by European Economic Association Committee of the Cabinet, 25 May 1960.

For some time, however, Macmillan continued to hold out the hope that EFTA might provide a 'bridge' to some form of association with the EEC – the FTA scheme by another name. But by the spring of 1960, economic and, especially, political considerations began to suggest to Macmillan that a radical departure might be necessary. A year on from that he had decided that he should seek British entry to the EEC. His skills as a political manager allowed Macmillan to persuade a reluctant Commonwealth and a sometimes doubtful Cabinet to follow where he had now decided to lead. With support from the United States and variable encouragement from an often imponderable France, the British made the historic decision to negotiate possible entry to the EEC in the summer of 1961.

4.1 Picking up the pieces

The first instinct of the British government towards the failure of the FTA proposal was to take what was called 'retaliatory action' against the Six. This soon mellowed into a less belligerent view, that measures of 'commercial self-defence' were required. What this meant in practice was that a free trade grouping of the 'non-Six' should be constructed so as to avoid British isolation in Europe and to prevent other states from being pulled into the EEC. In May 1959, the Cabinet approved the opening of negotiations which were to culminate in the creation of EFTA. Reginald Maudling, who had handled the FTA discussions and was to negotiate EFTA, later outlined Britain's objectives.

First, if freedom of trade in industrial products could not be expanded over the whole of Western Europe then it should be expanded as widely as possible. Second, there was a need for the European countries who were not members of the [European Economic] Community to organise themselves, because, otherwise the superior bargaining power of the Community would enable Brussels to pick them off one by one. Third, any organisation which was to be formed had to be of a character which would not serve to perpetuate the division of Western Europe, but which would rather provide a useful basis for future negotiations to achieve a wider European settlement.

Reginald Maudling, *Memoirs*, London, 1978, p. 74.

4.2   Taking stock

The Chancellor of the Exchequer, Derek Heathcoat-Amory, spelled out a similar message to the Cabinet on the day that the House of Commons approved the setting up of EFTA. Though the Chancellor attempted to put a brave face on things, the message was essentially pessimistic.

How serious is the potential economic damage to us of the Treaty of Rome? It would be unwise to draw conclusions too quickly, but there are three points that I would mention at once:–

(i) The position is greatly affected by what happens to the Seven. If we are able to hold the Seven together, this will limit the danger (and provide some gains to offset our losses). If, on the other hand, the Seven were to fall apart, and the rest of them inevitably come within the orbit of the Six, our position would be greatly weakened. The Six take one-seventh of our exports: the Six and Seven and peripherals take one-quarter.

(ii) It may be that the effect of the Treaty of Rome will be to make our problem of maintaining a satisfactory balance of payments during the next decade somewhat more difficult, and correspondingly somewhat to worsen our prospects of economic growth. But this depends very much on the policies of the Six and of the United States and of ourselves and the Commonwealth; and I think we must await a more thorough review. We must not forget that our economy is changing fast all the time; it has shown itself in recent years very adaptable, and we should not take a defeatist view.

(iii) The worst danger is that the Six might adopt policies which would make other countries revert to restrictive policies, and damage the whole fabric of international trade rules, leading to a general situation of quotas and tariffs and preferential arrangements which would be very bad for us indeed. Generally speaking, the consolidation of Western European economic power in the EEC inevitably reduces our influence in the formulation of the world trading rules and puts us at risk accordingly. It could likewise become a magnet tending to attract our industry and capital from the United Kingdom into Europe – and thus leaving us in a backwater. There is no certainty, and not necessarily a likelihood, that such damaging results would follow – but the possibility is there. These dangers, again, would be much greater if the Seven were to fall apart.

Public Record Office, London, CAB 129/99, C(59)188, memorandum by the Chancellor of the Exchequer, 14 December 1959.

4.3   EFTA as a bridge

> In his assessment to the Cabinet, Heathcoat-Amory was not optimistic that EFTA might provide a basis for negotiation between the Seven and the Six, and he advised that an agreement between the two groups 'may be unrealisable or at best ... we shall make very slow progress towards it'. This was not the Prime Minister's view, as this conversation between Macmillan and the Danish Prime Minister reveals. Here is an evident desire to reassure the Danes, who had doubts that an industrial free trade grouping would be helpful to their agricultural markets and thus were most in danger of being 'picked off by Brussels'; Macmillan also expresses his view of the Seven as another means to the same ends as the defunct FTA.

We had a very useful hour's talk about the proposed new European grouping – the Seven. I tried to persuade him (a) that I regarded this as a bridge, not an act of trade war against the Rome powers; (b) that I did not think that the Six would retaliate – many of our friends in the Six had expressed their pleasure at what was going on; (c) that we must not wait; and not try official negotiations with the Six until our organisation of the Seven was formed; (d) that he should send his Foreign Minister as soon as possible to negotiate with us on the agricultural problem on a *bilateral* basis.

Mr. Hansen was rather cautious at first. He seemed particularly anxious about possible retaliation by Germany and Italy against Denmark's agricultural exports. But he finally seemed to agree to all these propositions.

Harold Macmillan, *Pointing the Way 1959–61*, London, 1972, p. 52. The meeting took place on 12 June 1959.

4.4   The obstacle of the Paris/Bonn axis

Clearly, the hope survived in certain quarters that there was a chance of a deal with the EEC without having to join the Community. Maudling, however, like the Chancellor, was dubious and, like Heathcoat-Amory too, he saw the French as the source of the problem.

The fact is the French do not seem to want us in Europe at all. The Community of the Six has become a Paris/Bonn axis, with Paris at the moment the dominating partner on the basis of Adenauer's personal policy. The other four countries are really no more than satellites. While they may resent this, there is little they can do about it.

... I do not think, therefore, we can look to any fruitful resumption of negotiations in the near future. The French seem determined to treat the Germans, who have twice invaded them this century, better than they treat the British, who have twice fought by their side. Adenauer, who let you down very badly last year in the Free Trade Area, shows no sign of restraining his guilt complex to the extent of putting any pressure on the French. While we are entitled to express our resentment at this situation, I cannot see that any attempts at cajolement are likely to bring results.

... I remain convinced that if we were to reject the idea of forming some alternative association with our friends outside the Six we should be left without a friend in Europe and we should thoroughly deserve such a fate.

Public Record Office, London, PREM 11/2827, Maudling to Macmillan, 3 March 1959.

4.5   Persuade the French; bully the Germans

Even before the EFTA negotiations had been concluded, Macmillan's mind was turning towards the possibility of a British arrangement with the EEC which might go beyond an EFTA/EEC association. To obtain this he intended not to cajole the Germans, as Maudling had implied, but to threaten them. The French, in the meantime, would be coaxed.

Clearly one of the most important tasks of the next five years will be to organise the relations of the United Kingdom with Europe. For the first time since the Napoleonic era the major continental powers are united in a major economic grouping, with considerable political aspects, which, although not specifically directed against the United Kingdom, may have the effect of excluding us both from European markets and from consultation in European policy.

For better or worse, the Common Market looks like being here to stay at least for the foreseeable future. Furthermore, if we tried to disrupt it we should unite against us all the Europeans who have felt humiliated during the past decade by the weakness of Europe. We should also probably upset the United States, as well as playing into the hands of the Russians. And, of course, the Common Market has certain advantages in bringing greater cohesion to Europe. The question is how to live with the Common Market economically and turn its political effects into channels harmless to us.

We are erecting a first line of defence in the economic field through the Seven. But this, for geographical and other reasons, is a rather tender plant. We must no doubt allow the Seven to come into being properly before we make any further economic moves, but it seems desirable to set in train as quickly as possible a thorough examination of (a) the probable effects of the Common Market on our economy, (b) the sort of price it would be worth paying in order to be economically associated with it (something more in fact than just the concept of the Free Trade Area), and (c) the measures of defence which we might take....

All [the] economic work is more or less straightforward and could be put in hand. What is much more difficult is how to handle Europe politically. The core of the Common Market is the Franco-German Alliance. In the last resort it is the Governments of these two countries which we must influence. I suggest, however, that we may have to use different tactics in each case....

The French are not ... united about the political advantages to them of the European Economic Community; but all ... groups of French supporters of the Community have an interest in excluding the United Kingdom from it.

The Germans see the advantages of the Common Market largely in political terms. Dr. Adenauer, in particular, fears the effect of Soviet political pressure on an isolated Western Germany, and also believes that only a Franco-German political alliance can prevent the Anglo-Saxons from doing a deal with the Russians over Eastern Europe at Germany's expense. He is, therefore, prepared to pay an economic price for French political help....

Since the French are fundamentally in a very strong position politically, I believe that we shall not succeed in bullying them into accepting us as a partner in Europe; we shall have to coax them ... I do not believe it will be done only by fair words. We shall have to think of some deeds as well.... The Germans, however, are not in a strong political position, and I would have thought that there was some chance of bullying them. For example, when Dr. Adenauer comes here we might take the offensive a little about Anglo-German relations, pointing out that the Press continue hostile and that it is really difficult to expect them to take any other line when it appears that a European grouping is being created from which Britain is excluded even though we are the second largest defender of Germany.

Public Record Office, London, PREM 11/2985, Macmillan to Selwyn Lloyd (Foreign Secretary), 22 October 1959.

4.6   Thoughts on joining the Six

Macmillan's musings on 'something more ... than just the concept of the Free Trade Area' should be seen in the context of a more general shift in attitude towards the EEC. In the wake of the collapse of the FTA negotiations Heathcoat-Amory had listed the usual arguments against British membership of the EEC: Commonwealth connections, agricultural concerns, loss of sovereignty. These were still accepted as fundamental. Interestingly, however, the Chancellor also suggested that these might not be the obstacles they once were.

There are two points which were regarded as insuperable in 1955 but which might not be so to-day if all the Six were really anxious to include the United Kingdom and if on other grounds the United Kingdom wished to join –

(a) it was assumed in 1955 that if the United Kingdom were a member of a Customs Union we should have to put a tariff on Commonwealth goods, and this was clearly an insuperable obstacle. But in principle this is no longer the case. The Treaty of Rome implicitly includes the possibility of free entry – Eastern German goods into Western Germany, Tunisian, Moroccan and French overseas territories' goods into France. Whether the Six would agree to Commonwealth free entry is another matter; the scale of the Commonwealth problem is altogether different from the existing exceptions. And formidable origin problems would arise, even if the common tariff was tailor-made to suit us.

(b) We assumed in 1955 that the institutions of the Customs Union would be so supra-national that we could not accept them. We may not like very much the existing arrangements in the EEC, but they are far short of being supra-national.

Public Record Office, London, CAB 129/96, C(59)27, memorandum by the Chancellor of the Exchequer, 20 February 1959.

4.7 A cold wind from Washington

A severe blow to the British view of EFTA as an alternative system to the EEC and as a possible basis for future accommodation with the Community came from Douglas Dillon, American Under-Secretary of State, when he visited London in December. Dillon made it clear that the Eisenhower administration was prepared to tolerate the EEC as a discriminatory trading bloc because it offered the greater political advantages of cementing relations between France and Germany and strengthening Europe against Communism. The creation of the EFTA was, in their eyes, an unnecessary complication. If it remained entirely distinct from the EEC, it offered the unwelcome prospect of a divided Western Europe. On the other hand, an EFTA/EEC arrangement could be to America's economic disadvantage.

Mr. Dillon's visit did not result as well as we had hoped. The reports of his attitude in the *Times* and elsewhere were wholly misleading, and will of course have done damage in Europe. But nevertheless, it is clear that the United States do not regard a Seven/Six agreement as necessary (politically or economically) or desirable.

The attitude of Mr. Dillon may be summed up as follows:–

(i) The United States support the Six for political reasons, i.e. to see a strong and cohesive Power in Western Europe. They have always been prepared to accept disadvantages to United States trade in order to get this political objective. They do not see why the existence of the European Economic Community (EEC) should create a political split in Europe – all can work together, they say, in the North Atlantic Alliance (and of course in the Organisation for European Economic Co-operation (OEEC)).

(ii) The United States will press the Six with increasing strength to adopt a liberal trading policy – the more firmly established are the Six, the harder the United States will feel able to press. They would clearly welcome support from us and from the Seven.

(iii) Although unenthusiastic, the United States accept the Seven. When the European Free Trade Association (EFTA) Convention comes before the General Agreement on Tariffs and Trade (GATT) they will want to satisfy themselves that it is in accordance with the international trade rules.

(iv) The United States do not oppose in principle a Free Trade agreement between the Seven and the Six, provided that it is in accordance with GATT. But they do not positively want to see an agreement, because they see it as widening and increasing the discrimination against them and so they will not press the Six to come to agreement. They do not believe the Six will be prepared to negotiate anyway, until they feel stronger and assured that a wider European agreement would not frustrate the development of the Six....

Thus, we are bound to accept the fact that the prospects of any significant progress towards a Seven/Six agreement at any rate during the next few months are dim.

Public Record Office, London, CAB 129/99, C(59)188, memorandum by Heathcoat-Amory, 14 December 1959.

4.8 Changing course a little

Dillon's attitude to EFTA brought disturbing political aspects to the fore. If Washington favoured the EEC over EFTA, then the 'special relationship' with Britain stranded outside the Six was likely to wither, dissolving one of the principal foundations of British post-war foreign policy. The solution offered by the Foreign Secretary, Selwyn Lloyd, was for Macmillan to work as assiduously towards an Anglo-French partnership as he had to restoring Anglo-American friendship since Suez. The illusion remained that this could be achieved by Britain remaining outside the Six.

Towards the end of 1956 our minds were moving towards a closer relationship with Europe. That was the basis of the paper which I put to the Cabinet advocating a WEU nuclear effort.[3] Relations between Sir Anthony Eden and President Eisenhower had suffered a severe shock: Sir Anthony distrusted Mr. Dulles; it therefore seemed better to look towards the Continent....

When you became Prime Minister, however, a new opportunity presented itself with regard to the Americans because of your old personal relationship with the President. We therefore switched back from Europe and turned towards the United States, (driving our WEU allies in the process to accept reductions of 22,000 in our soldiers in Germany!). Throughout 1957/8 and 9, there is no doubt that this policy brought solid advantages to us.... This has been considerably due to personal relationships at the top.

The least satisfactory element in our relations has been the United States' backing of the Six and being so unenthusiastic about the wider European Free Trade Association or the Seven.

Looking ahead I feel that there are difficulties. These will increase with the next United States administration. Although we may still be regarded as the single most congenial ally, I believe that the Americans will think more and more of the Six as the group which they have to consult and whose views they must consider. With the strength of Communist China growing, the United States will be looking for tough allies and the Germans, the French and the Dutch within the Six seem to be that. We are always trying to hold them back or give them advice which seems to end in them not being able to do what they want to do.... With

[3] See 3.17.

some of those with whom we deal, I do not think the British arouse any more friendly feelings than the Germans or the French or the Italians. We are all difficult allies in our own particular ways.

In these circumstances, should we change course a little? We must preserve the best possible relations with the United States. We must do nothing to make them feel that we are turning away from them, or working against them. But should we now try to make the same sort of effort with France as we did in 1957 with the United States? Our assets are your personal relationship with General de Gaulle, the underlying French fear of Germany, and the fact that we do not really object to tripartite consultation which they want.[4] Against this would be French selfishness and the considerable dislike for us in certain quarters, but if we could get a situation in which the political views of the Six meant in practice the Anglo-French view, or an Anglo-French-German triangle, with Britain and France in agreement within it, it might prevent the diminution of our power to influence the Americans. The programme for the new *entente* would be:–

(i) to further our present line vis-a-vis the Soviet (which I think de Gaulle himself rather likes);

(ii) to keep Germany on the right lines, i.e. tied in as firmly as possible to us but less rigid towards East German contacts, reunification having been abandoned in the foreseeable future;

(iii) to reach a political settlement of the Sixes and Sevens somehow;

(iv) to guard against the Americans indulging in any disastrous enterprises in the East.

... I realise, of course, that the French will be less congenial, more selfish and therefore more difficult to work with than the Eisenhower administration. Our aim however should be over the next two or three years, to create a pattern in Anglo-French relations, which will have the result of the United States still reckoning with us and also prevent the Six becoming so rigid that they give the game to the Soviets in Europe and perhaps elsewhere.

Public Record Office, London, PREM 11/2998, Selwyn Lloyd to Macmillan, 15 February 1960.

[4] For 'tripartite consultation' see under 4.9.

4.9   Appeasing de Gaulle

Macmillan was increasingly aware of the political significance of coming to some arrangement with the Six.
This, he acknowledged too, meant finding some substantial
inducement to persuade de Gaulle. At a meeting with
ministers and advisers at Chequers in November he toyed
with an idea which was to recur frequently over the next
three years – giving de Gaulle access to nuclear technology.

It was suggested that some consideration be given to the possibility of saying to General de Gaulle that he should carry on with
the Six, that he should be given the bomb, that the WEU should
be brought to an end, that the UK should withdraw its troops
from Europe, and that we negotiate new alliances integrating
only the subjects such as radar, which did not make sense without
integration. It might be put to de Gaulle that we would be
prepared to act on these lines if he himself were in return to make
some concession, for example, to ensure that there were proper
economic consultation between the Six and the Seven....

There was further discussion on the possibility of making a
deal with de Gaulle on the basis of giving France the bomb by a
UK initiative. THE PRIME MINISTER thought this approach
should be considered as we should get nothing out of any
orthodox diplomatic approaches.

> Because there was no certainty that such an offer would
> influence de Gaulle, nothing was done. It would also cause
> difficulties with the Americans under the McMahon Act.
> Macmillan did, however, keep an eye open for ways in
> which an arrangement might be reached with the French. In
> September 1958 the General had published a memorandum
> proposing the revision of the NATO command structure to
> allow a tripartite Anglo-French-American predominance.
> This had not gone down well in Washington, and the
> British had, therefore, not supported it. To Macmillan's
> surprise, however, at a meeting of the Western heads of
> government at Rambouillet during December 1959,
> Eisenhower accepted the idea of 'clandestine' discussions on
> the French memorandum. This seemed a godsend to
> Macmillan, who now seemed able to offer an inducement
> to de Gaulle without offending the Americans.

116

I hope therefore – and I really do regard this as of vital importance – that we shall do nothing in private talks or arrangements
with the State Department to reduce the importance of the
position taken at Rambouillet or try to get out of it. If de Gaulle
thought that we were trying to get out of it he would not forgive
me and would change his whole opinion. When therefore the
French come forward with suggestions as to how the Rambouillet
agreement is to be carried out I hope we shall be forthcoming. If
there is any hesitation let it be the Americans and not ourselves. I
am quite entitled surely to work on what the President said and
proposed. It is not my object to pull him back because the State
Department think he may have gone too far. As for the reactions
in other NATO countries, I am not so much concerned about
that....

Now I come to the vital point. My purpose now must be to
support de Gaulle on the political front and his desire to join the
ranks of the Great Powers, and to encourage him to get the fruits
of his famous memorandum, and so forth. In return he must give
me the greatest practical accommodation that he can on the
economic front. The future of British trade in Europe is far more
important than whether a few French fighters are or are not put
under the command of SACEUR. If there is a global war the
fighters will be useless anyway. As we do not believe there will be
a global war, what is really important is British trade interests.

Public Record Office, London, PREM 11/2679, record of meeting
on 29 November 1959; Macmillan, *Pointing the Way*, pp. 113–
14, note from Macmillan to Selwyn Lloyd, 2 December 1959.

4.10   The deep crevasse

Despite this promising sign, two sets of talks with de
Gaulle, at Rambouillet in March and in London in April,
produced no substantial developments. Much worse was to
follow. The annual Commonwealth Prime Ministers'
conference in May, meeting in the shadow of the Sharpeville
massacre, was so divided over South Africa that Macmillan
feared that it might disintegrate. At the same time the Six
were pushing forward towards a common market by
reducing trade barriers between members, making a deal

117

with EFTA even more remote. On top of this, an East–West summit meeting in Paris in May collapsed following the interception of an American U-2 spy plane over Soviet territory. This was a triple blow. It was the wrecking of a meeting which he had personally stage managed, it demonstrated the relative impotence of Britain in the face of superpower animosity, and it reinforced for him the dangerous divisions which existed in Western Europe. 'We have fallen from the summit into the deep crevasse,' he commented.[5] His Private Secretary has remarked upon Macmillan's gloom after the summit had broken up.

> I never saw him more depressed. He was really cast down and glum after it. Apart from all the effort he had personally put into it, this was the moment he suddenly realised that Britain counted for nothing; he couldn't move Ike to make a gesture towards Krushchev, and de Gaulle was simply not interested. I think this represented a real watershed in his life.

Evidence from Macmillan himself suggests that de Zulueta's assessment was not an exaggeration.

> After the collapse of the Paris Summit I continued to argue with de Gaulle and Eisenhower that this tragic failure might soon bring us up against active Russian aggression. This made it all the more essential not to divide Europe. Meanwhile, my mind was turning more and more to the dangers of Britain remaining outside a community which controlled a central position in what was left of free Europe. But how was this to be done?

'Shall we be caught between a hostile (or at least less and less friendly) America and a boastful, powerful "Empire of Charlemagne" – now under French but later bound to come under German control. Is this the real reason for "joining" the Common Market (if we are acceptable) and for abandoning (a) the Seven (b) British agriculture (c) the Commonwealth? It's a grim choice.'

These, of course, were the somewhat exaggerated forms in which I recorded my passing thoughts. But they serve, perhaps, to show how, after careful deliberation, the decision taken a year later was made.

[5] Alistair Horne, *Macmillan 1957–1986*, London, 1989, p. 233, Macmillan to the Queen, 17 September 1960.

Alistair Horne, *Macmillan 1957–1986*, London, 1989, p. 231, Sir Philip de Zulueta to Horne; Macmillan, *Pointing the Way*, p. 316, including diary extract for 9 July 1960.

4.11 Political considerations predominate

> In the wake of the disappointment of the failed Paris Summit the European Economic Association Committee of the Cabinet, set up in March to look into Britain's relations with the EEC, accepted that joining the EEC was 'from a straight economic standpoint ... almost certainly ... the solution which would be most advantageous to the United Kingdom'. Most significant, however, was the Committee's assessment of the political impact on Britain if it did not enter the Common Market and the prospect of a reduced significance for the 'special relationship'.

The economic division of Europe will confront the United Kingdom with a most serious situation. There are significant political dangers which Ministers have emphasised in recent months – the fear that, despite the manifest advantages of the rapprochement between France and Germany, economic divisions may weaken the political cohesion of the West at a time when a common Western front is more than ever necessary. If, as seems to be the intention, the policy of the Six is to press forward with economic integration, impetus will be given to political integration. The Community may well emerge as a Power comparable in size and influence to the United States and the USSR. The pull of this new power bloc would be bound to dilute our influence with the rest of the world, including the Commonwealth. We should find ourselves replaced as the second member of the North Atlantic Alliance and our relative influence with the United States in all fields would diminish. All this would add to the strains on EFTA. The independence which we have sought to preserve by remaining aloof from European integration would be of doubtful value, since our diminished status would suggest only a minor role for us in international affairs.

Public Record Office, London, CAB 134/1820, EQ(60)27, 25 May 1960.

4.12 Avoiding 'hasty decisions'

The Cabinet discussed the work of the European Economic Association Committee on 13 July. It was a largely indecisive meeting with mixed views expressed and an overriding determination not to be rushed into making a decision. Though, at the end of the discussion, the British position was still to seek accommodation between the EFTA and the EEC, it was an important meeting in its tentative recognition that a step towards a British application to join the EEC on special terms might have to be taken. It is probably no coincidence that this hesitant Cabinet was restructured two weeks later.

The Chancellor of the Exchequer [Heathcoat-Amory] recalled that the Prime Minister had previously said that the Government would eventually have to choose between (i) initiating a dramatic change of direction in our domestic, commercial and international policies and (ii) maintaining our traditional policy of remaining aloof from Europe politically, while doing all we could to mitigate the economic dangers of a divided Europe. The report now before the Cabinet clarified the issues which would arise in making that choice. A decision to join the Community would be essentially a political act with economic consequences, rather than an economic act with political consequences. The arguments for joining the Community were strong. If we remained outside it, our political influence in Europe and in the rest of the world was likely to decline. By joining it we should not only avoid tariff discrimination by its members against our exports, but we should also be able to participate in a large and rapidly expanding market. However, the arguments against United Kingdom membership were also very strong. We should be surrendering independent control of our commercial policies to a European *bloc*, when our trading interests were world-wide. We should have to abandon our special economic relationship with the Commonwealth, including free entry for Commonwealth goods and the preferential system, and should instead be obliged to discriminate actively against the Commonwealth. We should have to devise for agriculture and horticulture new policies under which the burden of support for farmers would be largely transferred from the Exchequer to the consumer, thus increasing the cost of living. Finally, we should sacrifice our loyalties and obligations to the members of the European Free Trade Association (EFTA), some of which would find it impossible to join the EEC as full members....

The Chancellor said that his personal conclusion was that we should be ready to join the Community if we could do so without substantially impairing our relations with the Commonwealth.... In spite of the pressures for an early decision it would be wrong to be rushed into hasty action. We should try to carry our partners in the EFTA with us. We should also consult the principal members of the Commonwealth.... We should also try to find out what attitude the French were likely to take towards any proposal for membership on special terms or association. Finally, if it were ultimately decided to move in this direction, careful action would need to be taken to prepare public opinion in this country for such a move.

The President of the Board of Trade [Maudling] said that the Community was based fundamentally on the principle of com-mon policies, determined in common and carried out by a common institution. We should find it difficult to renounce our national control of policy, especially in respect of agriculture and commercial policies and our special relationship with the Commonwealth. On the other hand, the development of the Community was a serious economic threat to the United King-dom, as regards both our trade to Europe and our competitive position in the world. As our economic position declined in comparison with that of the Community, we should find that the United States and other countries would increasingly attach more weight to the views and interests of the Community.

In any negotiation with the Community we should have to seek an agreement which preserved the fundamental trading interests of the Commonwealth. It would, however, be disastrous to enter into negotiations until there was a political will in the countries of the Community to reach an accommodation with us. France and the United States held the key at the moment....

The Government should not allow themselves to be pushed into hasty decisions by the campaign in some parts of the Press. There was need of an authoritative statement in which the Government would make it clear that this was not a suitable moment for negotiations with the Community and, while expressing readiness to work towards a single trading system in Europe, would emphasise the fundamental objections to United Kingdom membership of the Community....

Discussion showed that the Cabinet fully agreed that the United Kingdom could not accept membership of the Community on the terms of the Treaty of Rome....

On the question whether the United Kingdom should seek membership of the Community on special terms, rather than remain outside it, it was argued that there was no ground for alarm that membership would commit us to close political integration. As a member, the United Kingdom would be able to influence the political development of the Community and strengthen the forces in it which already preferred a loose confederal arrangement. Although the time was not yet ripe for negotiations with the Community, we should prepare the ground for later negotiations by discussion with the other Commonwealth countries and the EFTA....

In further discussion it was suggested that the advantages of joining the Community and the dangers of staying outside had been exaggerated. Many other parts of the world besides Europe were expanding rapidly: and as a country with world-wide trading connexions we were in a good position to exploit these wider opportunities. To become a member of the EEC could be positively harmful to our position in the world, since some of the political and economic policies of the EEC countries did not inspire respect....

The Prime Minister said that it was important that the Cabinet as a whole should be kept closely in touch with the development of policy on this question ... a further authoritative statement of the government's attitude ... should explain that there were insuperable difficulties in the way of our accepting membership of the Community under the existing provisions of the Treaty of Rome, especially in relation to our responsibilities to the Commonwealth; but that we fully accepted the establishment of the Community and, with our partners in EFTA, would continue to seek for a mutually satisfactory arrangement between the EEC and the EFTA.

Public Record Office, London, CAB 128/34, CC(60)41, 13 July 1960.

4.13 Macmillan's 'grand design'

Evidence suggests that by the end of 1960 Macmillan was drawing near to a decision to seek British entry to the EEC. In the Cabinet reshuffle of 27 July, 'Europeanists' such as Duncan Sandys (Commonwealth), Christopher Soames (Agriculture) and Edward Heath (Lord Privy Seal) were given prominent positions. The disappointments of the early months of the year, indicating that accommodation with the Six was necessary, were followed by signs that this might also be possible. Visits to Bonn in August and Rome in July suggested that both the Germans and the Italians were as apprehensive as Macmillan about division in Western Europe and French domination of the Six. The incoming administration of John F. Kennedy in the United States might also present new opportunities. At the end of the year the Prime Minister drew up a lengthy, discursive, and somewhat downbeat summary of his thoughts on the existing situation, which became known as his 'grand design'. Essentially, this was Macmillan thinking aloud about the dangers presented by world Communism and Britain's role in helping the West to withstand this. Inevitably, this included his views on how the recent divisions in Western Europe might be brought to an end. This was, he believed, 'not primarily an economic but a political problem'. His objective was not yet decisively to move Britain into the EEC, but to find a formula to settle the 'Sixes and Sevens' issue. Again, this included the possibility of offering de Gaulle nuclear technology.

The Free World cannot, on a realistic assessment, enter on 1961 with any degree of satisfaction....

We are facing the monolithic strength of the Kremlin with a number of groupings, in Europe and in the Middle and Far East, which have nothing like the same unity of purpose or of practice.

Britain – with all her experience – has neither the economic nor the military power to take the leading rôle. We are harassed with countless problems – the narrow knife-edge on which our economy is balanced; the difficult task of changing Empire into Commonwealth (with the special problems of colonies inhabited by European as well as native populations); the uncertainty about our relations to the new economic, and perhaps political, State

123

which is being created by the Six countries of continental Western Europe; and the uncertainty of American policies towards us – treated now as just another country, now as an ally in a special and unique category.

We are faced with a complex of political and economic problems, affecting our relations with many nations and groups of nations. These problems are all intermingled. It is difficult to deal with them separately. Yet it is a tremendous task to attack them as a whole. So we are in danger of drift. Yet, if we are to influence events, we must not shrink from strong, and sometimes dramatic, action....

EEC and EFTA (Sixes and Sevens)
It is now pretty clear that an accommodation *could* be reached – which would at any rate reduce, and perhaps altogether eliminate the economic split in Western Europe.

It is equally pretty clear that it *will not* be reached, as things are going now. There will be talk – pleasant phrases – and no action.

The Germans, Italians, etc. would agree to one of the schemes now under tentative discussion. The French will not. The French means de Gaulle.

Yet, by a strange paradox, if de Gaulle were to disappear, an accommodation might be still more difficult. Whatever happened in France, there would be great confusion, perhaps even disintegration. French Federalist opinion would be strengthened (Monnet and all that) and timid Frenchmen would seek a refuge in a European Federal State. Difficult as de Gaulle is, his view of the proper *political* structure (Confederation not Federation) is really nearer to ours. If he wished us to join the political institutions it would be easier for us to do so if they took the form he favours.

If a settlement is not reached in the near future, the split will get worse and will become (again, from the point of view of our overriding aim – the joint struggle against Communism) dangerous and perhaps fatal. The economic consequences to Britain may be grave. However bold a face it may suit us to put on the situation, exclusion from the strongest economic group in the civilised world *must* injure us.

It must also injure the world, because economic exclusion must in the long run force us into military isolationism and political neutralism.

The triumph of the Federalists in Europe means, sooner or later, the triumph of the unilateralists and neutralists here.

We ought therefore to make a supreme effort to reach a settlement while de Gaulle is in power in France. If he gave the word, all the Wormsers[6] would turn at once. Why is he obstructing a settlement? How are we to deal with him? I am sure that a settlement can only be reached on political lines. Sixes and Sevens ... is now not primarily an economic but a political problem and should be dealt with as such....

France
... What do we want?
What does de Gaulle want?
How far can we agree to help him if he helps us?

(a) We want Sixes and Sevens settled
We must make it clear that we mean what we say – that if it is *not* settled, Europe will be divided politically and militarily.

We should have to denounce our liabilities under WEU.... It is obvious that the conditions which led to WEU have disappeared, and the basis on which we undertook these obligations has radically changed. *Then* France did *not* discriminate against British trade. *Then* France wanted British support against the danger of a renascent Germany. The first condition has gone. We assume that the French are happy about the second. Or *are* they? The French must judge.

(b) De Gaulle wants the recognition of France as a Great Power, or at least equal to Britain.
He suspects the Anglo-Saxons.

So long as the 'Anglo-Saxon domination' continues, he will not treat us as European, but as American – a junior partner of America, but partner....

De Gaulle feels that, while all this [NATO] machinery exists, the vital decisions are made – or not made – between the American and British Governments in Washington. De Gaulle feels that he is *excluded* from this club or partnership....

---

[6] Olivier Wormser, Director of Economic Affairs at the Quai d'Orsay and a prominent mouthpiece of the Gaullist position on Europe. See 5.1.

Can what *we* want and what *de Gaulle* wants be brought into harmony? Is there a basis for a deal?

Britain wants to join the European concern; France wants to join the Anglo-American concern. Can terms be arranged? Would de Gaulle be ready to withdraw the French veto which alone prevents a settlement of Europe's economic problem in return for politico-military arrangements which he would accept as a recognition of France as a first-class world Power? What he would want is something on Tripartitism and something on nuclear. Are there offers we could afford to make? And could we persuade the Americans to agree?...

Tripartitism
... If we could work out a plan ... based on de Gaulle's request of more than a year ago, which Eisenhower at one time accepted – and if we could sell it to the Americans, this would give de Gaulle at least one of his demands. He would have to know that it was *we* who had got it for him....

Nuclear
De Gaulle's second – and to him vital – ambition is the nuclear weapon.

Can we give him our techniques, or our bombs, or any share of *our* nuclear power on any terms which
  (i) are prudent and publicly defensible for us, at home, in the Commonwealth, and generally;
  (ii) the United States will agree to?
At first this seems hopeless. But since I think it is the one thing that will persuade de Gaulle to accept a European settlement – not merely in the economic field of Sixes and Sevens (which is vital), but in the general association of the British, with other Governments, in a Confederal system – I think it is worth serious examination....

I think we should give urgent study to this and see if we can devise a workable plan – which (at the right moment) we could get the United States to accept and which we could then use to win de Gaulle over....

What this memorandum tries to do is to call attention to the need to organise the great forces of the Free World – USA, Britain, and Europe – economically, politically and militarily in a coherent effort to withstand the Communist tide all over the world.

Public Record Office, London, PREM 11/3325, memorandum by Macmillan, composed 29 December 1960 to 3 January 1961.

4.14 Macmillan decides

It seems that Macmillan made his decision that Britain should apply to join the EEC somewhere around March 1961. In January he visited de Gaulle at Rambouillet and spoke to him of tripartitism and the nuclear issue. Everything now depended on the attitude of the Americans. In March George Ball, the American Under-Secretary of State for the new Kennedy administration, was informed while in London by Sir Frank Lee[7] and Edward Heath that Britain was 'perfectly prepared to accept the idea of moving towards some kind of [European] federation'.[8] When Macmillan visited Kennedy in April, to the surprise of at least one of his accompanying advisers, Robert Hall, this was repeated to the President.

On Europe, the PM was very eloquent and shifted the UK position quite a bit compared to anything I had heard before, or indeed then I thought was agreed, by the Cabinet or anyone else. The gist of what he said was that it was an American as well as a UK interest that the UK should be a full member in the political sense of the Treaty of Rome. Otherwise the desire of the French to put an end to 'Anglo-Saxon domination', and the deep desire of the Germans to show that they were strong and independent again, would lead in the end to a Third Force. But the PM wanted to know if the US agreed. He said that the French wanted the UK in but on Third Force lines whereas he (the PM) would never agree to anything that weakened the US–UK entente.

Alec Cairncross (ed.), *The Robert Hall Diaries 1954–61*, London, 1991, p. 265.

[7] Head of the Treasury.
[8] Michael Charlton, *The Price of Victory*, London, 1983, pp. 246 and 264.

4.15   The Cabinet debates

Kennedy was helpful over tripartitism but cautious over
sharing American nuclear technology with the French.
Macmillan decided to move forward anyway. Macmillan
now had to square this with the Commonwealth and the
country (especially the farming interest) without splitting
the Conservative Party. EFTA had also to be appeased. This
was skilfully managed. Though the farmers remained
recalcitrant, the Commonwealth states were dealt with
separately through visits by individual Cabinet ministers –
the St John the Baptists, as Macmillan called them. The
EFTA states were promised 'safeguards' and the public
debate remained deliberately muted. As this extract from
the Cabinet record shows, party loyalty was prevented from
fraying, initially at least, by the decision to negotiate the
possible terms of entry rather than entry itself.

The Commonwealth Secretary [Duncan Sandys] said that in the
three countries he had visited – Australia, New Zealand and
Canada – there were serious anxieties about the possible consequences of the United Kingdom's joining the EEC. They were
concerned about the changes this would involve in the trading
relationships with the United Kingdom; but they were even more
concerned about its political implications. They feared that an
economic union between the United Kingdom and the other
countries of Western Europe would lead in one way or another to
a political union which must weaken the Commonwealth
relationship. Canada also feared that this would draw her increasingly into the economic and political orbit of the United
States. He had tried to reassure all three Governments that, if a
wider political association became necessary, the United Kingdom
would be more likely to favour the larger concept of an Atlantic
union than any purely Continental system.... Despite their fears,
the other Commonwealth Governments had recognised that the
decision to enter into negotiations with the Community was
solely for the United Kingdom Government, for whom it was
much more important than themselves. They now expected us to
open negotiations, without further consultation, and would be
surprised if we did not do so....

The Minister for Aviation [Peter Thorneycroft] said that the
conclusion he had drawn from his visits to Commonwealth

countries in Asia was similar to those of the Commonwealth Secretary; that, so far as the Asian countries were concerned, their recognition that the final decision was for the United Kingdom left us free to enter into negotiations with the Community and they expected us to do so....

The Minister of Labour [John Hare] said that ... in the African countries, as elsewhere in the Commonwealth, there was the same understanding of our position and the same desire for close consultation at all stages.

The Minister of Agriculture [Christopher Soames] said that he had had discussions with the National Farmer's Union (NFU) and with other representatives of farmers in the United Kingdom. The NFU were taking the extreme line that the interests of United Kingdom farmers could be safeguarded only by continuation of the existing system of support.... Considerable opposition to our applying for membership must therefore be expected from the NFU, who would no doubt win much support from the farmers....

Summing up the discussion *the Prime Minister* said that it was evidently the view of the Cabinet that we should enter into negotiations with the EEC in order to find out on what terms they would agree to our joining the Community. A decision to negotiate was a very different matter from the later and much more critical decision to join the Community but, since a formal application to accede to the Treaty of Rome was a prerequisite of any negotiations on terms, the distinction might not be easy to make apparent to public opinion in this country and in the Commonwealth. A decision to negotiate might be more acceptable to our own public opinion if the emphasis were not all placed on the practical economic advantages (and the inevitable disadvantages of not doing so) but if some appeal were also made to the idealistic elements in British thinking. In announcing the decision it would be necessary to achieve a delicate balance between, on the one hand, creating the impression in the United Kingdom, the Commonwealth and EFTA that we had already decided to join the Community on whatever terms we could obtain and, on the other hand, suggesting to members of the Community that we had no real will to join them....

Public Record Office, London, CAB 128/35, CC(61)42, Cabinet meeting 21 July 1961.

4.16   The Cabinet decides

The following week the Cabinet took the plunge and accepted that negotiations, along the lines proposed by Macmillan, should be opened with the Six.

The Cabinet–

Agreed that a formal application to join the Treaty of Rome should now be made for the purpose of enabling negotiations to take place with a view to ascertaining whether the special needs of the United Kingdom, the other Commonwealth countries and the other members of the European Free Trade Association could be met.

Public Record Office, London, CAB 128/35, CC(61)44, Cabinet meeting 27 July 1961.

5

Out of the wilderness 1961–73

From the outset, it was recognised that the principal obstacle to Britain's application would be de Gaulle himself. Macmillan, with a fluctuating confidence that he could handle his old wartime associate, failed to prepare the ground properly. Despite three unhelpful personal meetings with the General during 1961 and 1962 – at the Prime Minister's home, Birch Grove House, and at the palaces of Champs and Rambouillet – Macmillan seems to have been genuinely shocked by de Gaulle's veto when it came in January 1963.

Harold Wilson, Prime Minister of a Labour government from October 1964, was faced with similar considerations to those which had confronted his predecessor. First of all, the Labour Party was divided on the question of joining the Six. In October 1962, after some havering, the then Leader of the Opposition, Hugh Gaitskell, in a speech to the Party conference, had condemned the terms of entry which Macmillan appeared to be negotiating. But to Labour in office, things looked less clear cut. Britain's balance-of-payments problem remained as intractable under Wilson as under Macmillan. One commentator sees 'the story of the years 1964–67 in large part the story of Labour's desperate attempts – in the end unavailing – to avoid having to devalue the pound.'[1] Certainly, the pattern of British economic growth looked depressing when compared with figures for most of the Community states. Increasingly, neither the EFTA nor the Commonwealth seemed likely bases for a British economic rejuvenation. The Commonwealth was also in some political disarray following the start of the Rhodesia crisis in 1964, while the 'special relationship' faltered owing to American dismay over Britain's failure to provide unequivocal support for the war in Vietnam.

[1] Anthony King, *Britain Says Yes: The 1975 Referendum on the Common Market*, Washington, 1977, p. 13.

At some point between 1964 and 1966 Wilson, until then opposed to entry into Europe, came round to the view that Britain should apply for membership of the EEC (or simply the European Community (EC) as it officially became after the merger of ECSC, Euratom and the EEC in 1965). Any overt change in policy was made politically dangerous by the divisions within the Labour Party on the issue and by the fact that between 1964 and the general election of 1966 the Labour government possessed only a tiny parliamentary majority. Once the latter problem had receded and Wilson had skilfully manoeuvred his Cabinet to agree to apply for membership, the spectre of a Gaullist veto re-emerged. For a time, Wilson, like Macmillan before him, convinced himself that he could persuade the General. A second veto of British membership, in May 1967, showed this to be an illusion and a third British attempt had to wait another three years.

The success of this third attempt was not entirely predictable. Attempts to work out transitional arrangements between Britain and some of its Commonwealth trading partners, the increased food prices for Britain which the running down of these and acceptance of the CAP would entail, plus questions of budget contributions to the Community remained among the major potential stumbling blocks. A crucial difference, however, was that by June 1970, when negotiations began, Britain had a Prime Minister, Edward Heath, who was determined to take Britain into the Community and France had a President, Georges Pompidou, who did not share his predecessor's stout resistance to this. A Treaty of Accession was signed on 22 January 1972 and, following a closely fought struggle for ratification in the Commons, Britain, at last, became a member of the European Community on 1 January 1973.

5.1 Macmillan and the French enigma

The most severe obstacle in the negotiations for British entry to the EC was likely to be de Gaulle. Macmillan's confidence either that the General would support the British application or that he could be induced to do so tended to vary. A major difficulty was trying to decipher what the French wanted. This problem had existed for some time, as Sir Frank Lee, Permanent Under-Secretary at the Treasury, noted of a conversation with his French opposite number, Olivier Wormser.

Monsieur Wormser clearly regarded this as an occasion for an agreeable general talk (the Washington scene; Africa; the general outlook in the UK; the latest work of Madame Simone de Beauvoir) rather than a discussion of the Six/Seven problem. When at last (at about 7.35 p.m.) I got him to speak on this he described to me the general lines of Sir Roderick Barclay's[2] exposition earlier in the day.... He said (this was in the closing minutes of our talk in the car) that it would make a great difference if only we would say definitely that we could join the Six. But when I said 'Yes, but does this mean that we can join and get our essential conditions in regard to say the Commonwealth and agriculture?' He smiled and said 'that, of course, is the $64 question'. And by that time we had arrived at our destination. It was an agreeable conversation, but I felt that I had rarely seen a more consummate display of playing all the bowling with a dead bat.

Public Record Office, London, FO 371/158170, minute by Sir Frank Lee, 27 February 1961.

5.2   The Emperor of the French

Macmillan had similar uncommunicative experiences with de Gaulle. Following an informal visit to Macmillan's home, Birch Grove House, the Prime Minister made this assessment of his guest.

The Emperor of the French (for he is now an almost complete autocrat, taking no notice of any advice and indeed receiving little of independent value) is older, more isolated, more sententious, and far more *royal* ... he is well informed, yet remote. His hatred of the 'Anglo-Americans' is as great as ever. While he has extraordinary dignity and charm, 'unbends' delightfully, is nice to servants and children and so forth, he does not apparently listen to argument. I mean this most literally. Not only is he not

---

[2] Deputy Under-Secretary in the Foreign Office.

convinced, he actually does not listen. He merely repeats over and over again what he has said before....

The tragedy of it all is that we agree with de Gaulle on almost everything. We like the political Europe (*union des patries* or *union d'états*) that de Gaulle likes. We are anti-federalists; so is he. We are pragmatists in our economic planning; so is he.... We agree; but his pride, his inherited hatred of England (since Joan of Arc), his bitter memories of the last war; above all, his intense 'vanity' for France – she must dominate – make him half welcome, half repel us, with a strange 'love–hate' complex. Sometimes when I am with him, I feel I have overcome it. But he goes back to his distrust and dislike, like a dog to his vomit. I still feel that he has *not* absolutely decided about our admission to the Economic Community. I am inclined to think he will be more likely to yield to pressure than persuasion.

Harold Macmillan, *Pointing the Way 1959–61*, London, 1972, pp. 427–8, diary entry for 29 November 1961.

5.3 The negative effect of long and difficult negotiations

At Birch Grove, Macmillan had urged de Gaulle 'not to think that the negotiations could drag on for a long time' as 'there would be a revulsion against the idea of allied unity, which could only damage the Free World as a whole'.[3] In fact, the British negotiating team, led by Edward Heath, did not begin its work until October 1961, and then proceeded only slowly in order to allow the Six, who were, in any case, preoccupied with setting up the CAP, to work out a collective response. At the same time, Commonwealth and domestic opinion became more restive. The difficulties and effect of this have been described by Sir Eric Roll, the deputy leader of the British negotiators, in conversation with Michael Charlton.

[3] Public Record Office, London, PREM 11/3338, Macmillan to Commonwealth Prime Ministers, 28 November 1961.

CHARLTON: To what extent was the negotiation with Europe also, in parallel – and at the same time, a negotiation with public and party opinion at home? That we are educating Britain itself – and that determined this step-by-step and very long process?

ROLL: But indeed, you've put your finger on a most vital point, which accounts both for the length of the negotiations and for their difficulty – because you were addressing a number of audiences at one and the same time. You were addressing your negotiators across the table, and the Press coverage was terrific. It had ready access to officials and ministers, so anything that was said in Brussels was very quickly and generally known. You were at the same time talking to the Commonwealth all the time, in London, to their representatives in Brussels, in the Commonwealth capitals and at collective meetings. You were talking to the farmers and the consumers. You were talking to the British public at large. You were talking to the House of Commons and the House of Lords. Each one required, if you like, a somewhat different presentation. I don't mean for any sinister reason but simply because their interests and concerns were different. When in Brussels you were being tough, you risked antagonising those at home you wanted to win over in the Cabinet and the House. When you were being too forthcoming in Brussels you were risking antagonising those who were expecting you to keep battling on all the time.

So, all in all this was a very, very difficult situation, and made it, of course, very easy for anyone who was really thoroughly hostile to the whole idea to play on that.

M. Charlton, *The Price of Victory*, London, 1983, pp. 265–6.

5.4 Public opinion shifts against British entry

As Macmillan had feared, tortuous negotiations allowed time for domestic opposition to British entry to the EEC to crystallise. Fuelled partly by Lord Beaverbrook's anti-EEC *Daily Express*, public opinion turned against British membership. This was especially worrying for a Cabinet which had come to view success in the negotiations as vital to the political survival of an increasingly unpopular government.

In discussion the following points were made:

(a) there had been a noticeable swing in public opinion in this country against United Kingdom membership of the Common Market. There had always been a body of opinion, particularly amongst farmers, which held that the advantages of membership must be doubtful until the conditions of entry were known; but more recently this had been replaced by a feeling, no doubt inspired by propaganda in the anti-Common Market newspapers and magazines that it would be wrong in principle for the United Kingdom to join the Common Market on any conditions. Up to now anxiety had centred on the effect on Commonwealth trade. But in the long run anxieties about the effect on our domestic agriculture might be even more important. It was among farmers that the propaganda against the Common Market seemed to be having most effect. It was significant that for the first time since the negotiations had started the President of the National Farmers Union was about to make a statement, which would be widely circulated, condemning in general terms the idea of British membership and paying no more than lip service to the fact that the issue would remain open until the precise conditions of our entry were known.

(b) Some apprehensions were also beginning to be expressed on religious grounds. It was being represented by some non-Conformist groups that the Common Market would involve a close association between a Protestant United Kingdom and a largely Catholic Europe. It would not be easy to deal with such allegations in public without risk of inflaming controversy in some quarters where sectarian feeling was still strong.

(c) It would be necessary for the Government to undertake as soon as practicable a campaign to present membership of the Common Market in a fairer light. This emphasised the importance of bringing the current negotiations to a conclusion as soon as possible.

(d) It might be of advantage if an early statement could be made about the legal consequences of our joining the Common Market. These had now been studied in detail and presented less difficulty than had been thought. An authoritative statement at an

136

early stage might restore a sense of proportion on this aspect of the problem.

Public Record Office, London, CAB 128/36, CC(62)44, minutes of Cabinet meeting, 5 July 1962.

5.5   Labour comes out against the negotiations

One important figure who became increasingly hostile was the Leader of the Labour Party, Hugh Gaitskell. Though there were enthusiasts for the European idea in the Labour Party, Gaitskell was not among them. He admitted as late as 1962 that he found the subject 'a bore and a nuisance'.[4] Until the summer of 1962, a mixture of a lack of personal conviction and a desire to avoid a Party split resulted in even-handed statements on the question of Britain's joining the Six. His stance was not, in fact, dissimilar to Macmillan's, and he regarded the central issue to be the political one of avoiding British isolation in world affairs. Between August and October 1962, however, Gaitskell was convinced that Macmillan had abandoned the position, which the Labour Party supported, of negotiating the terms of entry, and that he was determined to join the Community at any price. In a dramatic speech at the Brighton Party conference in October, Gaitskell accused the Conservatives of selling the Commonwealth down the river and endangering 'the end of Britain as an independent nation state ... the end of a thousand years of history.'[5] It was useful ammunition to de Gaulle's argument that Britain was not yet ready to enter Europe. Later Gaitskell described the reasons for his changed stance in a memorandum to President Kennedy.

[Right] up to mid-summer 1962 [the Labour Party] remained reasonably hopeful. I myself expected that the terms would be such as to prove acceptable to the Commonwealth Prime Ministers and that my task would be to persuade my Party to accept

[4] Philip M. Williams, *Hugh Gaitskell: A Political Biography*, London, 1979, p. 702.
[5] Williams, *Gaitskell*, p. 734.

them because they were by and large in accordance with our own conditions. I did not think it would be easy to handle the extreme anti-Marketeers, but I was prepared to do it as being the only course consistent with the line we had followed.... We were, therefore, bitterly disappointed and indeed astonished at the provisional agreements reached at the beginning of August....

I do not see how it can be seriously argued that these agreements in any way fulfilled either the Government's pledges or the Labour Party's conditions. Nor, indeed, have even the strongest pro-Market people in our Party ever suggested this. Had such terms been announced at the beginning of the negotiations, they would have been rejected out of hand by the British people.

Gaitskell to Kennedy, 11 December 1962, quoted in Philip M. Williams, *Hugh Gaitskell: A Political Biography*, London, 1979, pp. 712 and 724.

5.6   The question of the nuclear deterrent

At two uncomfortable meetings between Macmillan and de Gaulle at the Chateau de Champs and at Rambouillet (June and December 1962, respectively), where the usual difficulties over Commonwealth preferences and agricultural subsidies were raised, the General's interest in the possibility of Anglo-French co-operation over defence came to the fore. It may be that at these meetings the French gained the impression that Macmillan was willing to consider collaboration in the construction of a nuclear missile, though the records of the meetings provide no specific evidence that this was offered. In the months between the two meetings, however, the British had actively considered this as a possible means of persuading de Gaulle to end his resistance to their entry into the EEC.

But events overtook these considerations. Only days before Macmillan was due to meet de Gaulle at Rambouillet, Washington announced that the Skybolt missile, the American-built delivery system for Britain's nuclear warheads, was to be scrapped. Instead of pursuing some alternative arrangement with the French, Macmillan, at a tense meeting with President Kennedy at Nassau, persuaded the Americans to supply Britain with Polaris missiles, which would be pooled with the forces of NATO. That a 'European' alternative to this arrangement was available, and that Washington was not entirely trusted, is suggested by Julian Amery, Macmillan's Minister of Aviation.

I

The most striking thing about the talks are the General's apparent disillusionment with the idea of a political union of Europe and his almost open opposition to the idea of Britain joining the Common Market.

Was he saying what he really thought? Or was he adopting a bargaining position? Or was he simply probing and teasing in a way the Prime Minister sometimes does?

The theme which emerges again and again from the General's side of the conversations is that Britain will have to choose between America and Europe. She cannot have both, and the General still suspects that, in the crunch, she will choose America.

The only positive proposal that emerges, but it seems a vital one, is the General's statement that he would like to work with us on the development of missiles and other aspects of the deterrent. This is volunteered twice, once *tete a tete*, and once in a larger meeting.

II

The Polaris meeting is no doubt alright on paper. But it is reached against the background of a false prospectus on Skybolt and a determined attempt by the Administration to deny Britain a continuing independent deterrent.... It is all very different from the spirit in which the Skybolt agreement was reached with President Eisenhower.

It is difficult to feel complete confidence that the Americans will in fact deliver the missiles. At worst they may find a pretext for not doing so in the failure to build an effective multilateral force. At best we shall find ourselves tied even more closely to them in defence and foreign policy.

But is there an alternative to the proposed Polaris deal?

I am advised that British industry is capable by itself of developing a ballistic missile of either the Skybolt or the Polaris type.

This could be done by 1971/2. This involves a year or two longer than the American Polaris deal, but there are a number of ways of helping to bridge the gap that is going to face us anyway.

It would be expensive and a considerable strain on our human resources. But de Gaulle has suggested that he would like to work with us on missiles and other aspects of the deterrent. So we might expect a substantial French contribution to the ballistic missile programme and possibly to any stop-gap measures.

At the end of the day we should also have an effective ballistic missile industry in Britain and France.

III

If my advisers are right in saying that we are capable of producing a ballistic missile in eight to ten years there is anyhow the opportunity of putting de Gaulle to the test.

The Prime Minister might convey a message to him on the following lines:–

'My agreement with President Kennedy just safeguards the British independent deterrent. But it is hedged about with a lot of qualifications and will make me very dependent on the Americans at least until I have got the missiles. There is also always the danger that by 1968 or so I may be let down again as I have been over Skybolt.

The situation would be improved if you also accepted the proposal as we could then act together.

All the same it would be much more satisfactory if we could develop and produce our own missile, whether sea launched or air launched, and have it under our own control from the beginning.

At Rambouillet the other day you said you would like to develop missiles and other aspects of the deterrent with us. I now propose that we should select together the kind of missile we want to develop and produce it jointly, each of us retaining full independent control of the missiles when they are produced. We should also work together on the development and production of the delivery system.

You will realise that if I abandon the Polaris agreement with the Americans in favour of this proposal my relations with the United States will be seriously strained. I could only take this risk and in effect choose Europe as against America if you will now abandon your opposition to Britain's entry to the Common Market.'

IV

If de Gaulle says 'Yes', we shall be in the Common Market and will have a truly independent deterrent.

If de Gaulle says 'No' we shall have to stretch our existing deterrent as far as we can and either hope for Polaris or make a new missile entirely on our own.

Public Record Office, London, PREM 11/4230, Julian Amery's dictated response on reading a report of the Rambouillet talks, 27 December 1962.

5.7 De Gaulle's veto

> Macmillan did not go so far as Amery suggested, though he did propose that America might supply the French with Polaris missiles and the British provide them with nuclear warheads. It was too late. On 14 January 1963 came Macmillan's 'great and grievous disappointment'[6] in the shape of de Gaulle's press conference which vetoed Britain's entry to the EEC. It is debatable how far the veto was motivated by de Gaulle's resentment over the Polaris agreement. Agricultural differences, the imbalance which he considered Britain's entry would bring to the EEC, particularly because of its American connections, were each noted. But the Nassau agreement openly demonstrated British ties with Washington. This, and perhaps hopes dashed of a nuclear deal with the British, clearly rankled with de Gaulle.

Question What is France's position concerning the Kennedy multilateral formula, that is to say, concerning the Nassau agreements?

[6] Harold Macmillan, *At the End of the Day 1961–63*, London, 1973, p. 368, diary entry 4 February 1963.

Answer.... In the Bahamas, America and Britain concluded an agreement and we were asked to subscribe to it ourselves. Of course, I am only speaking of this proposal and agreement because they have been published and because their content is known. It is the question of constituting a so-called multilateral atomic force, in which Britain would turn over the weapons it has and will have and in which the Americans would place a few of their own. This multilateral force is assigned to the defence of Europe and is under the American NATO command. It is nevertheless understood that the British retain the possibility of withdrawing their atomic weapons for their own use should supreme national interest seem to them to demand it.

As for the bulk of American nuclear weapons, it remains outside the multilateral force and under the direct orders of the President of the United States. Furthermore, and in a way by compensation, Britain may purchase from America, if it so desires, Polaris missiles which are, as you know, launched from submarines specially built for that purpose and which carry the thermonuclear warheads adapted to them for a distance of 1,100–2,000 miles. To build these submarines and warheads, the British receive privileged assistance from the Americans. You know – I say this in passing – that this assistance was never offered to us and you should know, despite what some report, that we have never asked for it.

France has taken note of the Anglo-American Nassau agreement. As it was conceived, undoubtedly no one will be surprised that we cannot subscribe to it. It truly would not be useful for us to buy Polaris missiles when we have neither the submarines to launch them nor the thermonuclear warheads to arm them....

Extract from President de Gaulle's press conference held in Paris, 14 January 1963, in Uwe Kitzinger, *The European Common Market and the Community*, London, 1967, pp. 187–90.

5.8 Britain and the EC under Labour: the pro-Europe view

The Labour government which came to power in October 1964 with only a small majority was headed by an anti-Marketeer, Harold Wilson. By 1966 he was preparing his Cabinet for a second application. It is not clear when this conversion took place, partly because of Wilson's own

142

adroit political style, but also because he had to tread very carefully in order not to damage an already precarious government. A key pro-Marketeer was the Deputy Leader of the Party and head of the new Department of Economic Affairs, George Brown. Brown's views on Europe, as this extract from his memoirs suggests, were a mixture of the practical and the visionary, and reminiscent of Ernest Bevin's objectives.

Geographically, historically and in every other way the British are among the leading nations of Western Europe. I have always quarrelled with Dean Acheson's much-repeated remark about Britain's having lost an empire and not found a role. We *have* a role: our role is to lead Europe. We are, and have been for eleven centuries since the reign of King Alfred, one of the leaders of Europe. It may be that Britain is destined to become *the* leader of Europe, of Western Europe in the first place, and of as much of Europe as will come together later on....

It is our business to provide political leadership, to provide the stability that for so long has eluded the democracies of the mainland of Europe. I have as much arrogant patriotism in me as anybody else and I don't want to see Britain's becoming just one of a number of small European states. That is why I feel that we must support the idea of a united Europe, play our full part in bringing it about, and offer leadership wherever we can. I don't see where else leadership can come from other than from this country....

By bringing Western Europe together we should provide a domestic market of some 300 million people and be associated with countries whose economies are in many ways complementary to ours. That would give us an economic base big enough to stand up to anything that the Americans or the Russians can do industrially.

George Brown, *In My Way*, Harmondsworth, 1972, pp. 202–5.

5.9   The sceptical Labour view

Those Labour ministers who were opposed to joining the Six, on the grounds of tradition, economic cost, the loss of sovereignty, and the predominance of capitalist economics over socialist planning, were in frequent fear that Brown and his supporters, such as the Foreign Secretary, Michael Stewart, were engineering a drift towards Brussels.

Monday, January 31st 1966
I came up to London steamed up about the Cabinet paper which Michael Stewart had just circulated on de Gaulle's policies.... It seemed to me a crazy paper.... What it argued was we must regard General de Gaulle as the worst enemy in the world because of his wicked plan for knocking the supra-national elements out of the Common Market and for working with the Soviet Union to get an understanding over Germany's head. As I thought these were pretty sensible policies I agreed with Tommy[7] that I would try and scotch the paper.

So the moment I got into my office I got down to dictating a caustic memo to the Foreign Secretary. This is only the second time I have done this.... Now on this occasion I took good care to send copies of my memo to James Callaghan,[8] George Brown and also to Barbara Castle.[9] I organised the putsch on a relatively small scale because I did not want to create a Cabinet crisis, which there would certainly have been if everybody in Cabinet had been forewarned next Thursday. I was also aware that if I forced a straight vote on whether we should apply for entry to the Common Market or not, the pro-Marketeers would win. They have been pretty busy during the past few weeks. I learnt from Tommy that at the beginning of December Michael Stewart had approached the PM urging that we should make an immediate application to enter the EEC and this had only been frustrated when the PM point-blank refused the paper to be circulated. This had already aroused the wrath of Douglas Jay[10] and Fred Peart[11] who approached me over Christmas. So my memorandum was written and sent off....

Thursday, February 3rd 1966
Cabinet. When we got to item number two – as always, foreign affairs – I raised the issue of the Cabinet paper on General de

[7] Thomas Balogh, economic adviser to the Cabinet.
[8] Chancellor of the Exchequer and not a pro-European.
[9] Minister of Transport and an anti-Marketeer.
[10] President of the Board of Trade and an anti-Marketeer.
[11] Minister of Agriculture and an anti-Marketeer.

Gaulle. It went pretty well. We scotched the paper and Harold had to say in winding up that he personally sympathised with much of what I wrote in my memorandum. So our manoeuvre had succeeded.

Richard Crossman, *The Diaries of a Cabinet Minister, Volume One: Minister of Housing, 1964–66,* London, 1975, pp. 442–5.

5.10 Wilson and the EC

> The anti-Europeans were right to be nervous and, during his first fifteen months or so in office, a number of economic and political factors pushed Wilson towards a new stance on Europe. He was committed to developing Britain's technological industries, such as computing. But this was increasingly difficult to achieve in the face of a sluggish British economy and massive competition from American multinational companies. Europe, it could be argued, opened possibilities not offered by either the Commonwealth, increasingly seen as a declining asset, or the EFTA, now frequently viewed as a mistake. With federalism marginalised in a Gaullist Europe, membership also appeared more attractive. Even before the March 1966 general election, the result of which was greatly to strengthen Wilson's political hand, he appears to have begun to swing round to the idea of applying for EC membership.

Thursday, January 20th, 1966
George Brown to lunch. He was really at his best – warm, amusing, energetic. He was coming next Thursday but brought the meal forward, it appears in order to tell me that Wilson is deciding to enter the Common Market! He has obviously been moving in this direction for some months but this is a big leap forward. It is apparently due to the India–Pakistan agreement arrived at in Tashkent [concluding the 1965 India–Pakistan war] and the subsequent advice of John Freeman, our High Commissioner in Delhi. The Commonwealth provides no basis for a policy – so, into Europe.

> This may be an example of Wilson saying what his audience wished to hear. But a similar impression of a shift in policy is provided by Crossman a month later.

Saturday, February 19th, 1966
First, I predict that the date of the election will be Thursday, March 31st,[12] and that it will be announced by Harold when he comes back from Moscow.

Secondly, let me say that Harold expects to bring something back from Russia with him, some joint initiative on Vietnam, and he may be able to link this with a Common Market initiative. He has been under enormous pressure over the EEC from Stewart and George Brown ever since last December. He has been trying to get them out of their purely anti-French position; and it looks to me as though he is right in thinking that there are reasonable chances of a new approach to Europe. As he sees it, the difficulties of staying outside Europe and surviving as an independent power are very great compared with entering on the right conditions.

Cecil King, *The Cecil King Diary, 1965–70*, London, 1972, p. 56; Crossman, *Diaries of a Cabinet Minister, Volume I*, p. 461.

5.11 Barriers to entry

Deciding to join and being permitted to enter were quite different things. The Labour manifesto accepted the principle of Britain's entry into Europe so long as there were essential safeguards. But Wilson still had to overcome opponents to entry in the Cabinet. There were also serious practical issues. The state of the economy meant that a devaluation of the pound was a constant possibility. Wilson wished to avoid this on domestic political grounds. But there were those, including Brown and Crossman, who viewed it as a necessary preliminary to joining the EC. There was also the long shadow of de Gaulle.

Wednesday, May 25th, 1966
... At the NEC [National Executive Committee] in the morning at Transport House Brown gave a report on Europe. I will quote my notes in full because this seems to me an important meeting. George Brown said, 'If I am asked when in fact in terms of

---

[12] This proved to be correct.

present probabilities we could get into Europe, the answer would be "Never". But the question isn't about our getting into this Europe. The issue is whether we should get into a new trans-formed organisation or stay outside it.' Then he listed quite fairly the main difficulties. Firstly, we would be outside Europe until General de Gaulle was out of the way. Secondly, the crisis with France about NATO had to be resolved or got over.[13] Thirdly, we had to get our own economic situation under control. As of today entry to Europe would require devaluation. The fact that we are coasting along without any expansion of the economy makes entry impossible. Having listed the obstacles very clearly, he then added, 'Still, it's a good thing to make friendly noises.' If he'd said this publicly it would have been thought a complete about-turn from what he has been saying on his journeys around Europe. But it is true to George Brown's character. He regards propaganda as a substitute for action. All his life is salesmanship and he seldom waits for any solid achievement before beginning to boast of it. I think this is what has happened in the case of Europe. George Brown wants to get in and he also thinks that the less chance we have of getting in the more we must shout about it to fill in the vacuum.

Crossman, *Diaries of a Cabinet Minister, Volume I*, pp. 527–8.

5.12   Moving closer to application

In fact Brown – and Wilson – were more determined upon entry than Crossman allowed. Brown, Foreign Secretary after August 1966, was anxious to have Britain in the EC before 1969, in the hope of influencing arrangements for the CAP, which was due to come into operation in that year. In early 1967 Wilson and Brown visited the capitals of the Six for informal talks. This was clearly a step towards application, but Wilson was able to give the impression to doubters in the Cabinet that he was on hand to curb a possibly overenthusiastic Foreign Secretary. The sceptics were also able to comfort themselves with the view that,

[13] In March 1966 de Gaulle withdrew France from the institutional structure of NATO.

whatever Britain decided, the reality was that de Gaulle had not altered his view. Wilson and Brown, on the other hand, when they visited Paris in January came away convinced 'they had made an immense impression on the General'.[14]
Tuesday, 21 March, 1967

The first of our Cabinet discussions on Europe. We had before us the report by Harold and George on their European tour, plus a full account of each individual meeting at the time. Harold stressed that this first meeting should not try and take any decisions: we must not rush this crucial matter. The first thing was to get the facts clear on the points of difficulty we saw about going in. The main ones were the Common Agricultural Policy (CAP), capital movements and the Commonwealth, particularly New Zealand and the sugar agreement. Other difficulties had diminished as the tour proceeded e.g. regional policies presented no problem ... and any loss of European investment would, in his view, be offset by increased American investment here once the road to Europe was open. Even the sterling issue had been clarified. Nor had de Gaulle raised the special relationship with America. The big problem was that France did not wish to surrender her dominant position in the Community, and the Five would not in the last resort risk disrupting the Six in order to stand up to her.

George tried to urge that 1969 was a crucial year when policies in the Six would be reconsidered and that, if only we could get in, even the CAP would be renegotiable, but we didn't let him get away with that and forced him to agree that only the level of prices and the size of the import levy (as well as Britain's share of the Community pool) would be negotiable. The CAP would stay ... Dick [Crossman] and Denis [Healey] made a great deal of Kiesinger's[15] interview in *Der Spiegel*. Didn't this show that Germany was not prepared to press France to accept us and so we were wasting our time? Harold insisted that what Kiesinger said for publication was bound to be along these lines; privately he had indicated that he would certainly bring pressure. But in

[14] Crossman, *Diaries of a Cabinet Minister, Volume II*, entry for 21 March 1967, p. 285.
[15] Dr Kurt Kiesinger, Chancellor of West Germany.

any case, said Harold, don't let's get on to judgments at this stage. Let's stick to an objective examination of the facts under the three headings I have outlined.

And so, skilfully, he kept the temperature down and got us going through the details of the CAP. Some of us stubbornly refused to believe that, even if we were in on the price and other negotiations as members in 1969, we should ever be able to persuade these agricultural protectionists to bring farm prices down.... After two and a half hours it was decided we needed more papers for the next meeting ... Dick pressed for us to have the long-promised papers on the possible alternatives like the formation of a North Atlantic Free Trade Area or going it alone. Harold agreed that these must now be prepared. And so we parted amicably.

I thought Harold had manoeuvred brilliantly. I remain convinced he is anxious to get in (we are obviously not going to have any draconian Socialist measures from this Cabinet) and he had succeeded in guiding us into a discussion of details which is more effective than anything else in making principles look less important.

Barbara Castle, *The Castle Diaries, 1964–70*, London, 1984, p. 236.

5.13 The second veto

Richard Crossman estimated on 1 May that Wilson had a majority of sixteen to seven in the Cabinet on Europe. The Prime Minister had, in effect, worn down the anti-Marketeers: 'Just boring our way in,' Tony Benn complained to Barbara Castle.[16] On 2 May a Cabinet decision was taken to apply for membership of the EC. Divided among themselves, there were no resignations from the anti-Marketeers, though Douglas Jay, President of the Board of Trade, appears to have attempted to instigate like-minded colleagues to follow him in threatening to do so. Despite his superb tactical achievement, however, Wilson had underestimated de Gaulle's resistance to British entry as seriously

[16] Castle, *The Castle Diaries*, entry for 13 April 1967, p. 242.

as had Macmillan before him. A visit to the General in June, appropriately at Versailles, failed to win him over, and at a press conference on 22 November the British application was rejected. The economic emphasis which de Gaulle gave to his decision cruelly underlined the fact that Wilson had finally been forced to devalue the pound four days before.

To speak only of the economic field, the report communicated on 29th September by the Brussels Commission of the six Governments shows absolutely clearly that the Common Market is incompatible with Great Britain's economy as it stands, in which the chronic balance of payments deficit is proof of its payment imbalance and which, as concerns production, sources of supply, credit practices and working conditions, involves factors which that country could not alter without modifying its own nature.

The Common Market is also incompatible with the way in which the British feed themselves, as regards both the products of their agriculture, subsidised to the highest degree, and the foodstuffs purchased cheaply everywhere in the world, particularly in the Commonwealth. This rules out the possibility that London may ever really be able to accept the levies laid down by the financial regulation, and which would be a crushing burden on Great Britain.

The Common Market is further incompatible with the restrictions imposed by Great Britain on exports of capital which, on the contrary, circulates freely among the Six.

The Common Market is incompatible with the state of Sterling, as once again highlighted by the devaluation, together with the loans which have preceded and are accompanying it; also the state of Sterling which, combined with the Pound's character as an international currency and the enormous external debts weighing on it, would not allow the country to be part of the solid, interdependent and assured society in which the Franc, the Mark, the Lira, the Belgian Franc and the Florin are brought together.

Under these conditions, what would be the outcome of what is called Great Britain's entry into the Common Market? And if one wanted to impose it, in spite of everything, it would obviously mean breaking up a Community that was built and operates according to rules which do not tolerate such a monumental exception.

Nor could they tolerate the introduction as one of its leading members of a State which, owing precisely to its currency, its economy and its politics, is not at present a part of the Europe which we have begun to build.

Extract from President de Gaulle's press conference, 27 November 1967, from Uwe Kitzinger, *The Second Try: Labour and the EEC*, Oxford, 1968, pp. 314–15.

5.14   Edward Heath's approach to Europe

The Conservatives returned to power in June 1970 with Edward Heath as Prime Minister. The European question did not play a significant part in the general election campaign. This probably reflected low public interest in, even hostility towards, the issue following de Gaulle's second veto and also an attempt to douse antagonism towards Europe, which existed especially on the right wing of the Conservative Party. On 30 June, however, and only twelve days after taking office, the Heath government had entered negotiations with the Six on the basis of Labour's application for entry, which was still regarded as 'on the table'. The same economic arguments which had convinced Wilson also spurred Heath. More than this, Heath had been a supporter of European co-operation since the Schuman Plan, and had made his maiden speech in the Commons in favour of British participation in the Plan. Though framed to an audience at the Royal Academy, the speech below indicates that as Prime Minister he retained an emotional attachment to the European idea as a civilising influence rare in a British political leader.

'The artists, the writers, and the musicians have shown the economists and the politicians the way. We have to bring to the creation of European and economic unity the same creative effort, the same interplay of ideas and aspiration, the same ability to share our achievements that enabled them to make a reality of European cultural unity.'

He went on to say that if we could build Europe as a city at unity in itself, that had peace within its walls and plenteousness within its palaces, then it would be a place where the arts flourished and were honoured, a place where artists could live and work, a place where men could sing the merry songs of peace to all their neighbours.

'It is no mean or selfish objective which we seek. It is a noble ideal, long established in the traditions of European thought and well worthy of the aspirations of our generation. When we achieve our ambitions then history will indeed know that the spirit of man has at last triumphed over the divisions and dissensions, the hatred and the strife that plagued our continent for a thousand years. Humanity will be grateful that our European civilisation, to which it already owes so much, will be able to flower afresh in unity and concord.'

The Times, 29 April 1971.

5.15   Unsure about the French

Though there had been indications for some time that EC members other than the French – the 'friendly five', as they were sometimes known – were well disposed towards British entry, this goodwill had never been sufficient to overcome opposition from Paris. Even after de Gaulle's resignation in April 1969, doubts remained about the French position. Heath went out of his way to distance himself from the notion of a 'special relationship' with the USA. Also, Commonwealth issues had by this time been reduced to the, still contentious, matters of providing protection for New Zealand dairy farmers and West Indian sugar producers. However, the tough negotiating stance of de Gaulle's successor, Georges Pompidou, raised concerns that the new President either was expecting to squeeze new concessions from Britain, especially over the status of sterling as a reserve currency – which the French did not want – or was building up to another veto.

As he left the conference hall, one veteran who had sat through the first round of British negotiations 10 years ago said he had the nightmare impression of having heard the whole thing before....

France's new approach to the Common Market negotiations has convinced leading politicians in Brussels, Paris and London that – at least for the time being – President Pompidou wants to keep Britain out.

In the view of these observers France's tougher line at last week's talks on British imports of Commonwealth sugar – described by diplomats in the Community as 'mean', 'stingy' and 'obstructive' – plus her sudden demand that the status of sterling be placed on the agenda, amount to an effective veto.

It is argued that the hopes of Mr. Heath and Mr. Rippon, Britain's chief negotiator, for a quick deal before the summer recess, have certainly been stalled by these tactics.... Barring a highly improbable French change of heart, Mr. Heath must decide whether to persevere or cut his losses.

The Observer, 21 March 1971.

5.16 Determined upon success

Pompidou was, in fact, open to persuasion. Pressure from the 'friendly five' and French apprehension that under Willy Brandt Germany was taking a more independent line than under any other post-war Chancellor seem to have been important factors in leaning the President towards widening the EC. The CAP had now been settled in France's favour and the entry of Britain would mean that it would have to help pay for it. The cost of the CAP did not dampen Heath's resolve to get Britain into the EC and in direct, secret discussions with the French he and Geoffrey Rippon assured them that sterling would present no problems of compatibility with the currencies of the Six. In return, they received promises of interim support for the products of New Zealand and the West Indies. By June, Rippon, reporting on the formal EC discussions in Luxembourg to the House of Commons, even felt able to present British budget contributions to the EC in a favourable light.

I now turn to arrangements for our participation in the Community's budgetary system.

Here the arrangements which we have agreed would provide for a maximum annual contribution to be paid by the United

Kingdom in the first five years amounting to 8.64 per cent of the Community's budget in 1973, rising to 18.92 per cent of the Community's budget in 1977. Before the end of 1977 the Commission would calculate the contribution which the United Kingdom would have made in 1977 had we then applied in full the Community's budgetary system. On the basis of this calculation, a limitation would be applied to our contribution for a further two years, namely, 1978 and 1979, to ensure gradual progression to our full final contribution.

The House will want to know how the resulting contributions would compare with the estimates which I gave to hon. Members on 16th December when we made our initial proposals. The estimates of the budget of an enlarged Community have been revised downwards substantially since last year. At that time, it was thought that the budget of the enlarged Community might grow to a figure of $4,500 million in 1977. However, the butter mountain of which we heard so much at that time has melted, and agricultural prices in the Community have risen very little over the past four years, while world prices have gone on rising. The price gap, and consequently the cost of agricultural support in the Community, have accordingly fallen. The budget is now expected to grow from $3,300 million in 1973 to $3,800 million in 1977.

These sums are important ones. But the House will recognise that the Community has made arrangements which would be very satisfactory to this country on a number of other issues during the meeting which I have just attended, particularly on New Zealand. It is fair and right that this country should, if it joins the Community, play its proper part in all aspects of Community policies and developments.

There is still plenty of work to be done ... but the agreements reached in Luxembourg mean that we have now broken the back of the negotiations. We have been able to progress so far because the Community has demonstrated its political will to see the Community enlarged and to have Britain as a full member with it.

United Kingdom Parliamentary Debates, House of Commons, 5th Series, Volume 819, London, 1971, 24 June 1971, cols 1608–10.

5.17 'No ... erosion of essential national sovereignty'

The British public was now bombarded with governmental statements expounding the advantages of joining the EC. This appears to have had some impact for, according to opinion polls, public opinion swung over to favour entry. However, concern to sell the government's message may be responsible for a tendency, as in this extract from a White Paper of July 1971, to exaggerate to economic benefits offered by entry and to play down the issue of sovereignty.

The Political Case

If the political implications of joining Europe are at present clearest in the economic field, it is because the Community is primarily concerned with economic policy. But it is inevitable that the scope of the Community's external policies should broaden as member countries' interests become harmonised. That is the Community's clear intention. As regards the co-ordination of foreign policy, the practical obligations which the United Kingdom will assume if we join now will involve no more than we have already assumed in WEU. But we will be joining at a moment when we shall be able to influence the process of development. This will also be true of progress towards economic and monetary union. No firm timetable has yet been agreed for this in the longer term; the immediate steps agreed so far will not involve practical difficulties for us. If we were not to join this would not stop the Community of Six moving forward in both economic and political fields. Thus the options open to future British Governments would be limited without their having any say in the matter.

We shall have full opportunity to make our views heard and our influence felt in the councils of the Community. The Community is no federation of provinces or counties. It constitutes a Community of great and established nations, each with its own personality and traditions. The practical working of the Community accordingly reflects the reality that sovereign Governments are represented round the table. On a question where a Government considers that vital national interests are involved, it is established that the decision should be unanimous.

Like any other treaty, the Treaty of Rome commits its signatories to support agreed aims; but the commitment represents the voluntary undertaking of a sovereign state to observe policies which it has helped to form. There is no question of any erosion of essential national sovereignty; what is proposed is a sharing and an enlargement of individual national sovereignties in the general interest....

The Economic Case

The Government is confident that membership of the enlarged Community will lead to much improved efficiency and productivity in British industry, with a higher rate of investment and faster growth of real wages.... A more efficient United Kingdom industry will be more competitive not only within the enlarged Community but also in world markets generally. These improvements in efficiency and competitive power should enable the United Kingdom to meet the balance of payments costs of entry over the next decade as they gradually build up. The improvement in efficiency will also result in a higher rate of growth in the economy. This will make it possible to provide for a more rapid improvement in our national standard of living as well as pay for the costs of entry.

Cm 4715, The United Kingdom and the European Communities, London, 1971.

5.18   In with reservations

In the summer of 1972 a series of parliamentary debates on the Treaty of Accession, which had been signed six months earlier in Brussels, went in Heath's favour. Britain was to become a member of the EC from 1 January 1973. The significant debate, however, had already taken place over six days in the Commons in late October 1971, after which there were 356 votes for and 244 against entry. The heat being generated over the issue in party political circles, if not among the population at large, which was largely unasked and uninformed, is reflected in the diverse reactions of the popular press to the vote which followed the six days of debate in October. The two papers quoted were at opposite poles on the question of Europe and shared almost equally between them nearly eight million readers.

A mistake – a great mistake – has been made. But it has been made by the House of Commons, and the *Daily Express* accepts the verdict of the freely elected British Parliament.... So, if Britain has to go into the Market, then the Market must be fashioned to Britain's will ... and the *Daily Express* will champion British interests more fervently than ever before.... From today onwards the *Daily Express* will discharge its obligations – *by promoting* the British case in season and out, in Brussels, in Bonn, in Rome, Paris or London, wherever it is at hazard ... the *Daily Express*, the Voice of Britain, will be stronger than ever when it speaks to foreigners on behalf of Britain.

The Daily Express, 29 October 1971.

Dateline Westminster, October 28th
Time: 22.16 hours
The historic decision is made
YES TO EUROPE!! majority: 112

Front page, *The Daily Mirror*, 29 October 1971.

6

Half-hearted Europeans 1973–94

On joining the EC sixteen years after the Treaty of Rome, the British did not make a conspicuous effort to be congenial partners. This was not because Britain was unique in expecting special treatment. All the EC states sought to use the Community to pursue their own national objectives. However, in Britain's case self-interest was coupled with a marked lack of commitment to Community developments largely absent among the original Six or those new members which joined alongside or after the British (with the possible exceptions of Denmark and later Greece). A signal which Britain sent out to its European partners, more or less consistently over twenty years, was either that an error had been made in joining the EC, which could only be rectified by withdrawal, or that, now reluctantly a member, the Community must be shaped to Britain's particular image of it.

The tone was set by the Wilson government's renegotiation of Heath's terms of entry to the EC during 1974–75 and the consequent referendum on Britain's continued membership. From 1975, when Heath was replaced as Leader of the Conservative Party by Margaret Thatcher, the Conservatives progressively began to lose the claim to be regarded as the 'Party of Europe'. Thatcher took on the question of British budgetary contributions to the EC with a vehemently nationalist style, which sometimes obscured the justice of the British case and reinforced their image as resentful Europeans. Her vigorous resistance to a new flush of enthusiasm for further European integration which emerged in the Community during the 1980s was a considerable irritant to Britain's partners, failed to halt this process, and contributed significantly to Thatcher's own political eclipse. In contrast, her successor, John Major, felt the need to assert that Britain's place was 'at the heart of Europe'. But, in fact, Major had no more enthusiasm for further integration than had his predecessor. More than this, he was troubled by a vociferous wing of the Party which preferred a return to Thatcher's confrontational posture towards the Community. In an attempt to damp down this domestic disquiet, Major negotiated certain 'opt-outs' for Britain from some of the central clauses of the 1991 Treaty of Maastricht, which sought to translate the EC into the European Union (EU).

6.1 Contrasting British approaches to Europe

Heath was unfortunate in that he took Britain into Europe at a time of a world economic crisis, accelerated by the decision of the oil-exporting countries to double the price of their principal source of revenue during 1973. This adversely affected relations between Community members, and made it hard for the Conservative government to convince domestic opinion that joining the EC had been the best option for Britain. When a minority Labour government won the general election of February 1974, it was again deeply divided on Europe. Though neither of the two leading figures in the Party, Harold Wilson and James Callaghan, had much enthusiasm for the details of European integration, both felt that Britain's long-term future lay in the Community. They were faced with a core of pro-Europeans, principally on the right of the Party, and an anti-European group, mainly on the left. As in 1967, Party unity was Wilson's priority, and the 1974 election manifesto promised to renegotiate the terms obtained by the Heath government in 1972. By pledging, among other things, to seek a reform of the CAP, reassessment of the British contribution to the EC budget, and guaranteed freedom for British regional policies, Wilson hoped to appease the pro-Marketeers. The underlying threat that if agreements satisfactory to Britain were not forthcoming Britain would withdraw from the Community was intended to fend off the anti-Europeans. Nicholas Henderson, then British ambassador to West Germany, compared the differing approaches of the first two governments after Britain joined the EC.

1973

HEATH VISITS GERMANY

10 MARCH

The financial situation had ... stultified the whole purpose of the heads of government meeting because, far from being able to devote themselves to the future of Europe or how to give Europe a new dimension to bring about European union in the next few years, they had really been so held down by the present crisis that they had not been able to lift their eyes to the distant horizon at all. The elaborate briefings for the Prime Minister on what to say about regional policy, how to deal with the United States of America, or how to create and then conduct policy towards the Mediterranean – none of these subjects had been dealt with except in the most cursory way and then only in the margin of the financial problem. The meeting could not therefore be said to have succeeded in its original purpose.

1974
CALLAGHAN WEEK
24 MARCH
BONN

This has been Callaghan's week for me. The problems inherent for officials when they have to adapt themselves to a new government have been rendered even greater than usual by the arrival in power of a party bent on reversing the foreign policy of its predecessor. Heath's government made Europe the focus of its foreign policy. This in itself has been something of an innovation given the traditional blue water tinge of our diplomacy. It did more than change course. It took the lead, or at any rate Heath did, in stressing the need to create a European union governing all aspects of relations. At the summit meeting in 1972 Heath, Pompidou[1] and Brandt[2] declared that this union was to be achieved by 1980. Now, only two years after this resounding declaration, the new Labour government has made it clear, through the mouth of their Foreign Minister, Callaghan, that it does not accept this concept of union at all. Indeed it will only accept the customs union and common agricultural market aspects of the Community; and it will only accept these if the terms for Britain's membership are renegotiated to give Britain more financial benefit.

---

[1] Georges Pompidou, de Gaulle's successor as French President.
[2] Willy Brandt, Chancellor of West Germany.

Callaghan has left no doubt of his agnosticism about the idea of union if this means going beyond the limited economic sphere which I have defined above. Agnosticism is his own description. He has said that he intends to pursue a more traditional type of British diplomacy. He has told the [Foreign] Office that 'he wishes to put more muscle into the United Nations'; he attaches great importance to the Atlantic Alliance and he wishes to have closer relations with the Commonwealth. He favours global rather than regional solutions, and America is, of course, vital to any global approach. Europe comes after this and the policy towards it is to 'renegotiate British entry to the EEC in keeping with the Labour Party's manifesto'. He takes it for granted that we officials know that it is our duty to implement the manifesto and nothing but the manifesto.... His hope is that the outcome will be an agreement that will enable Britain to stay in the EEC.

Heath's decision to throw in our lot with, and indeed help to lead, Europe was widely welcomed on the Continent. It fitted in with the conviction, common amongst most modern European leaders, that if Europe is to stop tearing itself apart and to play the role and exert the influence on the world stage that its talents and tradition deserve, this can only come about if the countries join closely together in all aspects of life, political and economic. The new government's complete reversal of this policy looks like causing concern to our continental neighbours. I think that many of the leading members of the British Cabinet are unaware of this, or would scarcely care even if they were aware. Peter Shore, for instance, Secretary of State for Trade, does not conceal his intention to work for withdrawal from the EEC by negotiation.

Nicholas Henderson, *Mandarin: The Diaries of an Ambassador 1969–1982*, London, 1994, pp. 58–60.

6.2   The view from the left of the Labour Party

In part a reaction to the 1967 humiliation at the hands of de Gaulle and also in response to a pro-European government under Heath, the Labour left had reverted to its view that the EC was merely a 'capitalist club' which was essentially against the interests of the British worker. A leading light of the anti-Europe left was Tony Benn, Secretary of State for Industry and Minister of Posts and Telecommunications in the new government, who had become a convert to the anti-Market cause in the early 1970s out of a belief that the Brussels bureaucracy was chipping away at political accountability and therefore at sovereignty itself. A weakness of the left's case, however, was that its alternative of Britain standing alone had been tried and found wanting by successive post-war governments.

Monday, 25 March 1974

... I worked on my box and came to a third item of gloom for the day: the way in which the Common Market re-negotiations are being handled. Night after night I get a note that there is to be a meeting of the European Coal and Steel Community at which the British Steel Corporation is to be represented, or that there is to be a meeting of the European Postal and Telecommunications Ministers or a meeting of the Committee on Research in Science and Technology. Always, the Department says we should go to safeguard British interests, to adopt policies that are in our interest, and to show willing. Each time I say that I am against that and each time I am over-ruled. I was over-ruled today by the Foreign Secretary [James Callaghan] in a minute which said I couldn't control steel prices because it might bring the Commission or the European Court into action against us. One can see how democracy is completely undermined, once officials start getting together, and there is no proper ministerial or democratic accountability at the top. The more I see the Common Market from the inside, the more I want Britain to get out of it and live on its own, cooperating with others but not in any way bound by treaty obligations: a loose, joint harmonisation arrangement, perhaps linked to a customs union, that is all we need.

Tony Benn, *Against the Tide, Diaries 1973–76*, London, 1990, p. 128.

6.3 The left outmanoeuvred over renegotiation

This extract from the diaries of Barbara Castle, Social Services Secretary in the Wilson Cabinet, gives a flavour of the tensions in Cabinet which renegotiation produced and some indication of the deftness of the Wilson/Callaghan strategy of presenting the left with piecemeal 'victories' over the European Commission.

Thursday, 21 November 1974
... Fred [Peart][3] has come back from Brussels, flushed with what he considers a satisfactory deal over beef and sugar, but which some of us can see as the thin end of the wedge of capitulation over one of our major negotiating objectives: the transformation of the CAP. The discussion confirmed my worst fears. Fred pleaded that these had been the hardest negotiations he had experienced and we all murmured sympathy. But that was the whole point: we had had to fight like hell even to produce a dangerous compromise. His great triumph, he said, was that he had got the got the variable premium on beef.[4] There had been great hostility, but they had conceded in the end 'for a period'. In return he had had to concede some temporary intervention.[5]

Peter [Shore][6] came in first being one of the few people who has the knowledge and time to find his way through the agricultural complexities. He began by congratulating Fred on what he had achieved: variable premiums were guaranteed prices in disguise. But the difference was that the benefit was not passed on to the consumer. And he deeply regretted we had accepted any intervention, because this weakened our position for the long-term talks ... Jim[7] was positively nasty to Peter: 'He has got it utterly wrong. Fred has got deficiency payments accepted. This is a breakthrough in the ideology of the Commission.' And he added that of course we had to pay for our own variable premiums, 'and so we should'.

---

[3] Minister for Agriculture.
[4] A subsidy payment to farmers which varied with the market price.
[5] That is, EC intervention to buy surplus produce.
[6] Secretary of State for Trade, and President of the Board of Trade.
[7] James Callaghan, Foreign Secretary, and in charge of the renegotiations.

This jerked me into speech. I am now convinced that Jim is heading for a patch-up deal to stay in – and is actively pursuing it. I said his speech had alarmed me more than anything else. We had made no inroads at all on the CAP. The Community remained as opposed as ever to deficiency payments. All we had been allowed was 'a little private sin provided we paid for it'. 'Don't you *want* to amend the CAP?' snapped Jim. 'I want to abolish it', I retorted. Otherwise we should be saddled with all its disadvantages and would have to pay for any improvements we made to it through our own help to farmers. I warned that the real crunch was still to come and we had better not live in a fool's paradise.... We then turned to sugar, with which the beef deal is, of course, intertwined. On this, the more I listened to Fred's explanation the more convinced I became that here too we were heading for modifications of the Community policy which would merely mean that Britain remained enmeshed in it, while having to pay through the nose for any national improvements she wanted to make. But the rest dropped their opposition and the beef/sugar deal was agreed. Afterwards, as I sat next to Peter on the front bench, he said gloomily that he didn't like the way things were shaping at all.

Barbara Castle, *The Castle Diaries, 1974–76*, London, 1980, pp. 229–30.

6.4 The right and the referendum

Wilson had another strategy to deflect the left. In their manifestos for both the 1974 general elections, in February and October, Labour promised that there would be a chance for the nation to make a choice on membership of the EC once terms had been renegotiated. With Wilson's position strengthened considerably after October, the final decision was taken to test public opinion, not by yet another general election, but by a referendum. This was favoured by the left, indeed was pressed by Tony Benn, as opinion polls indicated a victory for the anti-Marketeers. Roy Jenkins, Home Secretary and a leading pro-European who had resigned from the shadow Cabinet two years earlier on the issue, remained firmly against a referendum for reasons similar to Benn's. Even before the October election, however, he had lost the battle.

On 16 September [1974] we had a day-long Cabinet/National Executive Committee meeting on the [general election] manifesto. I argued against the absolute commitment to the referendum and got quite a surprising amount of support, but not quite enough. The concession Wilson and co. made to me was to use the phrase 'consult the British people through the ballot box' rather than to flaunt the red cloth of 'the referendum' in my face. But it was a distinction without a difference. I therefore said that I would not do any early national press conferences.... It was not a question of pique but of the fact that they would lead to nothing but embarrassment, even more for the party than for me. Wilson had the sense to accept this quietly, but the egregious Hayward[8] blustered to me on the telephone saying that Shirley Williams[9] was making no difficulty at all about appearing.

The difficulty she made was not about appearing but, with her spontaneous honesty, what she said when she got there. Three days later, sharing the platform with Wilson, she suddenly blurted out (the right phrase according to those present) that if the referendum produced a negative result she would resign from the Government, resign from Parliament and retire from politics. This was the major headline of the day, which displeased Wilson far more than my non-appearance. The spotlight then turned on me. Would I stay if Mrs. Williams went? I was never much in favour of hypothetical commitments, but the issue having been raised I could not dodge it. When I went to Birmingham for nomination the next morning I therefore issued the following statement: 'My conviction that it would be a major mistake to come out of Europe is just as strong as Mrs. Williams's. I hope and believe that the negotiations can succeed, but naturally I would not stay in a Cabinet which had to carry through such a withdrawal, damaging for the world and doubly so for the country in its likely economic consequences.'

Roy Jenkins, *A Life at the Centre*, London, 1992, p. 389.

---

[8] Ron Hayward, General-Secretary of the Labour Party.
[9] Secretary of State for Prices and Consumer Protection.

6.5   The renegotiation 'victory'

Wilson's hope was to be able to present the renegotiation to the country as a success, and use this as the base for a yes vote in a referendum. With the latter set for June 1975, it was important to conclude the discussions with the EC beforehand. This was achieved at a European summit in Dublin on 10–11 March. In fact, as Jenkins put it, the renegotiation 'had more of cosmetics than reality about it'.[10] There was never any intention of pressing a redraft of either the Treaty of Rome or the Treaty of Accession. With the support particularly of Helmut Schmidt of West Germany and Valéry Giscard d'Estaing of France, who wanted to see Britain stay in the EC, some minor agricultural concessions were arrived at and a rather more important agreement to ease Britain's budget contributions. As for the Labour left, as eight years before, they were worn down by tedium. At the start of the important two-day Cabinet discussion on 17–18 March, after which agreement was reached to recommend a yes vote in the referendum, Barbara Castle was 'bored before we start' and considered the discussion a 'tedious charade'.[11] Even Tony Benn's more dramatic account suggests that the referendum was to be somewhat anticlimactic.

Tuesday, 18 March 1975
A momentous day in the history of Britain – the day of the Cabinet decision on Europe, the day of the parliamentary decision, the day of the dissenting Ministers' declaration....

At Cabinet we had before us the papers detailing the renegotiation package, and for the first time the issue of sovereignty was discussed properly. The crucial question was whether the Community was to be a supranational structure or a community of sovereign states....

I said ... 'This is the most important constitutional document ever put before a Labour Cabinet. Our whole political history is contained in this paper. It recommends the reversal of hundreds of years of history which have progressively widened the power of the people over their governors. Now great chunks are to be handed to the [European] Commission. I can think of no body of

[10] Jenkins, *A Life at the Centre*, p. 387.
[11] Castle, *Castle Diaries, 1974–76*, p. 340, diary entry for 17 March 1975.

men outside the Kremlin who have so much power without a shred of accountability for what they do ...'.

Michael [Foot][12] spoke. 'We are being asked to accept everything we opposed when we were in Opposition. Take tachographs as an example – we opposed them, but they have still been imposed on us. We are conniving at the dismemberment of Parliament. We are destroying the accountability of Ministers to Parliament, and if we elect a European Parliament by 1978 it will destroy our own Parliament....

Jim [Callaghan] said that it was not the first time that a document of this importance had been before a Labour Cabinet. It was all set out in the 1967 White Paper. Sovereignty of Parliament was not an issue, it wasn't even in the Election Manifesto.

This led to a protest from Michael who said that what was at stake was the draconian curtailment of the powers of Parliament. Harold [Wilson] pointed out that Michael was quoting from the February Manifesto. So Michael said that the phrase 'authority of Parliament' was used in the October Manifesto. 'Well', said Wilson, 'these are the differences between the old and the new testaments.'...

Harold Lever[13] commented 'Tony Benn is a legal pedant,' and debates on whether this was irrevocable were silly. The decision to withdraw would be disastrous.

Harold Wilson said, 'The British Parliament has the power to come out at any time.'

I asked if he'd be prepared to say that publicly.

'We can discuss that later,' he replied, 'when we come to the handling of the statement.'...

Harold then brought us on to the main question. Should we accept the terms or not? 'I recommend that we should stay in and that is the view of the Foreign Secretary, though he will speak for himself. We have substantially achieved our objectives, the Community has changed *de facto* and *de jure*. The attitude of the Commonwealth has changed too. The Commonwealth wants us to stay in, and the Commonwealth trade patterns have regrettably changed. If we had a free trade area for the UK, the conditions upon us would still be stiff or stiffer. I am only persuaded 51 per

[12] Secretary of State for Employment.
[13] Chancellor of the Duchy of Lancaster.

cent to 49 per cent, indeed I had anxieties right up to the last few days, but now I recommend that we stay in.'

Jim Callaghan followed, 'In supporting you, Harold, I would like to say something about the development of Europe. I am unashamedly an Atlanticist, but we are living in a regional world and we must use the regional organisations....'

I made my final speech. 'Prime Minister, I fear that the Cabinet is about to make a tragic error, if it recommends that Britain stays in. I recognise that Jim has done his best and probably got the best terms that are compatible with continuing membership. But we have not achieved our Manifesto objectives and indeed we did not even try.'...

The real case for entry has never been spelled out, which is that there should be a fully federal Europe in which we become a province. It has never been spelled out because people would never accept it. We are at the moment on a federal escalator, moving as we talk, going towards a federal objective we do not wish to reach....

Denis Healey[14] said that it would be a mistake to present the issue as Michael Foot and Tony Benn had suggested. The consequences outside would be serious, and economic problems were more important. He said this was a matter of judgment and a choice between evils. The Commission was set by the Treaty of Rome and it would have been better if we had been in there at the start....

So, in the end, it was sixteen to seven for staying in. Harold then said, 'I hope that nobody will think the result has anything to do with the way I composed the Cabinet because when I formed it a year ago, there were eight for Europe, ten against and five wobblies. Now, of those who have expressed their view, who intends to take advantage of the agreement to differ?'

Six of us said Yes – myself, Barbara, Michael, Willie,[15] Peter, and Eric.[16]

Thus it was that the Cabinet reached its view to stay in the Common Market.

Benn, *Against the Tide*, pp. 342–9.

---

[14] Chancellor of the Exchequer.
[15] William Ross, Secretary of State for Scotland.
[16] Eric Varley, Secretary of State for Energy.

6.6   Post referendum

From early 1975 there was never much doubt that the referendum, held on 5 June, would produce a verdict to stay in the Community. Possibly influenced by publicity over the 'success' of renegotiation, public opinion had reverted to a positive view of the EC. With an endorsement from the Prime Minister and the government for a yes vote, and with a group of perceived mavericks which cut across party boundaries urging no, the pro-Market vote in a poll with a high turn-out was over 68 per cent. But apart from the central fact that Britain had decided to remain inside the Community, little else had changed. The Callaghan government (1976–79), when it felt able, continued to resist what were seen as encroachments from Brussels – no matter how small.

Friday, 11 June 1976
… After lunch we came on to the EEC passport and a number of maroon passports had been handed round with the British crest and the words 'European Community' on the front. Peter [Shore] jumped in, 'We don't have to have these passports, do we? Surely we can keep our British ones if we want.' It emerged that this was another deal that Wilson had done and Peter could not keep his old one. He was boiling with rage. 'My children and grandchildren *forced* to abandon the old British passport!'

I joined him. I feel inordinately angry about this. Bruce Millan[17] said most people in his constituency didn't have passports and it was just a middle-class sentiment. In the end it went through, so in due course we are going to have a flimsy maroon passport. I shall renew mine before then.

Benn, *Against the Tide*, p. 579.

6.7   The European Monetary System

Callaghan, as well as being 'unashamedly an Atlanticist', was also hampered by presiding over a government with no overall majority, which was dependent upon Liberal

---

[17] Secretary of State at the Scottish Office.

support and also facing serious economic problems. In addition, as seen above, he had to cope with grumbling from the anti-Marketeers. Not surprisingly, Callaghan's line on Europe was a cautious one. A commitment, inherited from the Wilson renegotiation, to direct elections to the European Parliament met resistance in his own Party and difficulties with the Liberals, who wanted voting on the basis of proportional representation. This meant that the elections did not meet the deadline and the process had to be postponed for a year throughout the EC. More significantly, perhaps, Callaghan resisted moves towards monetary union which emerged from the Community.

This had first been proposed in December 1969, at a European summit meeting in The Hague, but had evaporated under the impact of the world economic recession which came in the wake of massive increases in oil prices during the early 1970s. By mid-1978 monetary union was again on the Community agenda, with the French, and especially the Germans, putting forward the idea of the European Monetary System (EMS) as a pathway towards Economic and Monetary Union (EMU). This staging post towards economic union allowed for an exchange rate mechanism (ERM) within which exchange rates could be adjusted to allow development towards a common currency and also a European Currency Unit (ECU), which, some expected, would eventually become this common coinage. Because of his personal inclinations and domestic concerns, Callaghan felt unable fully to subscribe to the new development and, though the EMS was functioning by 1979, Britain, uniquely at that time, stayed out of the ERM but allowed sterling to join other currencies in backing the creation of the ECU.

As a pro-European and President of the European Commission from 1977 to 1980, Jenkins's account is not entirely non-partisan, yet it does make pertinent observations on British attitudes after entry to the EC.

London I had not been to (officially) since 2 November [1978], when I formed the impression that Callaghan was not coming in [to the EMS]. But I was not absolutely certain. He seemed genuinely torn in his own mind, and almost plaintively asked why Giscard, without a very strong economy, did not seem to hesitate over taking the risk. I suppressed the desire to say, 'Because he does not suffer from the British disease of never co-operating fully', which might have been counter-productive, and replied, 'Because France is much more self-confident than Britain. They believe they can make a success of things, whereas we don't.' Callaghan said perhaps this was right. It was also the occasion, quoted by me in several subsequent speeches, when Callaghan vehemently denied that he was staying out because of political difficulties at home, and insisted that if he was convinced it was right for Britain he would come in whatever the political problems. 'But,' he added, 'I am nervous of being locked in at too high a rate of exchange, which will prevent my dealing with unemployment'. This animadversion was like a scissor-blade, which is of no interest without its pair. This companion was however splendidly provided by Mrs. Thatcher six months later when I saw her almost immediately after her election – in the same room to add to the symmetry. She assured me that she was in principle in favour of full participation in the EMS but was 'nervous of being locked in at too low a rate of exchange which will prevent my dealing with inflation.' In fact under both of them Britain enjoyed for several years a higher rate of un-employment and inflation than any participating country. But at least we remained bipartisanly faithful to our national habit of never joining any European enterprise until it is too late to influence its shape. Then, when wholly predictably, we are eventually forced to apply for membership, we complain bitterly that the shape suits others better than it suits us.

Jenkins, *A Life at the Centre*, pp. 483–4.

6.8 The BBQ

It has been suggested that Callaghan agreed to the proposal for the EMS only because he was given to believe that this new development would be matched by a reassessment of Britain's contribution to the Community budget. The British budget question (BBQ) was a long-standing grievance which had been glossed over during the Heath negotiations on British entry and subjected to a stopgap solution at the time of the Wilson renegotiation. The Community budget was based on revenues from imports from outside the common external tariff, plus 1 per cent of each member's receipts from value added tax. Britain was hit by this in three ways. It imported more from outside the Community that any other member state. Thus, Britain was contributing more to the budget than other members with stronger economies. However, as the highest cost to the Community budget was the CAP, the British saw a smaller return for their input than more agriculturally based countries in the EC.

Callaghan lost office before he could resolve the problem. Margaret Thatcher, who became Prime Minister in May 1979, tackled the BBQ with vigour, laying out her demands at the European Council at Strasbourg six weeks after her election victory and following this through at the Dublin and Luxembourg summits.

29 November 1979, Dublin
The Council started at 3.40 in Dublin Castle and went on until 8.10. There was a certain amount of routine stuff introduced by us [the European Commission] first, which lasted longer than I expected (some, I think, were rather keen that it should do so). Then into the budget question about 6 o'clock, introduced briefly by me [as President of the Commission]. Mrs. Thatcher did quite well for once, a bit shrill as usual, but not excessively so. There was quite a good initial response. The Italians and the Irish, for instance, offered to pay their share and it was agreed without much question that we should fully apply the financial mechanism.

Schmidt started to cross-question me on how we could do things beyond that, which was difficult but not impossible. Then towards the end Mrs. Thatcher got the question bogged down by being far too demanding. Her mistake, which fed on itself subsequently at dinner and indeed the next morning, arose out of her having only one of the three necessary qualities of a great advocate. She has nerve and determination to win, but she certainly does not have a good understanding of the case against her (which was based on the own-resources theory, or theology if you like), which means that the constantly reiterated cry of 'It's my money I want back', strikes an insistently jarring note. 'Voilà parle la vraie fille de l'épicier', someone ... said. She also lacks the third quality, which is that of not boring the judge or the jury, and she bored everybody endlessly by only understanding about four of the fourteen or so points on the British side and repeating each of them twenty-seven times.

Monday, 28 April 1980, Luxembourg
When the Council eventually assembled, we met from 12.20 to 3.40. To sit this long was again I think a mistake.... We got down to the BBQ straight-away and Mrs. Thatcher was certainly being much quieter, less strident, less abrasive, than at Dublin. Early on Schmidt brought forward a proposal which was very good for 1980: the British deficit should not be allowed to grow in that year beyond the average for 1978 and 1979. This opened up in my view a great opportunity for Mrs. Thatcher, though it obviously still left the 1981 position open. But later in the discussion Giscard made the proposal that in 1981 the payment to offset the British deficit should be the same as the 1980 figure. This, on top of Schmidt's proposal, had the effect of giving the British a complete guarantee for 1980 against uncovenanted increases....

I suggested at this stage that we might have an adjournment, which I thought would have been useful, and one or two people took it up, but Mrs. Thatcher unwisely did not press for it.... Had she been able to sit back and consider this – talk to her advisers, to Carrington[18] and perhaps to me – we might have made some progress....

I lunched with the others.... Mrs. Thatcher did not appear, being closeted with British ministers and officials, but then came back at 5.00 and refused it. One or two attempts at *nettoyage*[19] were made but she remained adamant. I had told her before that I thought she was making a great mistake by not accepting, and she good-temperedly but firmly said, 'Don't try persuading me, you know I find persuasion very counterproductive.' So when she had spoken I said in the Council I thought she was making a major error, that it was a substantial offer, and that we were splitting Europe for a difference which was very small compared with the original gap.

Roy Jenkins, *European Diary 1977–81*, London, 1989, pp. 528–9 and pp. 592–3.

---

[18] Lord Carrington, Foreign Secretary.
[19] That is, clearing things up.

6.9   The Fontainebleau agreement

As Jenkins points out, the cost of Britain's contribution to the EC budget was relatively small and far less than, say, Britain's own defence budget. This, however, was not the point so far as Thatcher was concerned. Apart from the strength of the British case, which allowed Thatcher to project a high-profile patriotic stance to her domestic audience, cutting the cost of 'Europe' dovetailed completely with her political philosophy of reducing public expenditure. This meant that she was not interested in short-term refunds but wanted a more permanent restructuring of the Community's budgetary system in a way which made it more equitable to Britain. With admirable tenacity she held out against the other EC states until agreement was reached at the European Council held at Fontainebleau in the summer of 1984. An enlarged EC (Greece was admitted in 1981 and Spain and Portugal were to enter in 1986) increased the cost of running the Community, which Thatcher was able to exploit in her demand for efficiency and reform. Fontainebleau was widely regarded as a triumph at home, and the compromises necessary to achieve it (e.g. an increase in the percentage of VAT receipts to the Community) were played down. The cost of five years of often bitter dispute between Britain and its EC partners was significant, and the lessons learned from the experience, as Nigel Lawson[20] suggests, may not always have been the right ones.

A considerable advance on the Dublin offer was secured at meetings in Luxembourg and Brussels in the spring of 1980, where rebates were negotiated for 1980 and 1981 worth £1,570 million in all. This success was due entirely to the obstinacy of Margaret Thatcher who was reluctant to accept even this improved offer, although she did in the end. She was right in thinking that this agreement, which went only up to the end of 1981, did not mark the end of the matter. A third rebate of £476 million for 1982 was also secured, accompanied by a Community commitment to find a permanent solution. This was finally concluded at the Community Summit in Fontainebleau in June

[20] Chancellor of the Exchequer, 1983–89.

1984, where Britain won a £600 million rebate for that year plus an automatic formula for refunds in subsequent years. If Margaret's bloody-mindedness was the essential ingredient, the successful outcome owed a good deal to the skill of the lean and cerebral Michael Butler, Britain's Ambassador to the Community, whose understanding of the nuts and bolts of Community law and practice was as impressive as his unflagging zeal in carrying out his remit.

There was, however, a negative aspect to Margaret's triumph. Although the quality improved later on, the poor advice given by the Foreign Office over the Community Budget in 1979 and 1980 reinforced Margaret Thatcher's instinctive distrust of that Department; and the wetness of the diplomatic service became a perpetual theme in her thinking. Moreover, the outcome of the Budget negotiations persuaded her that it always paid to be bloody-minded in dealings with the Community. This was to prove increasingly counterproductive in practice. Nor did it help when I sought to interest her in sterling's membership of the Exchange Rate Mechanism (ERM) of the European Monetary System (EMS).

Nigel Lawson, *The View From Number 11: Memoirs of a Tory Radical*, London, 1993, pp. 110–11.

6.10   A resurgence of 'Euro-idealism'

The struggle over the BBQ, while demonstrating Thatcher's confrontational style on Europe, also indicated that there were those in the Conservative Party who would not let her entirely have her own way on relations with the Community. Indeed, Fontainebleau, the scene of her greatest victory on EC matters, also hinted at developments which were to become increasingly uncomfortable for the Prime Minister over the following months. One phase of her dealings with Europe was now, more or less, over. The next – trying to cope with a resurgence in the Community of what she dismissively called 'Euro-idealism' – was about to begin.

[At the European Council at Brussels, March 1984] I had not expected such a totally negative outcome [on the BBQ]. So the question immediately arose as to whether we should withhold payments to the Community budget. This was partly a legal and partly a political question. We had always been advised that if we withheld contributions we would almost certainly lose any subsequent case before the European Court. In this instance, however, we were on somewhat stronger legal ground because the Community was withholding rebate payments to which we were entitled by previous agreement. Probably, we would have lost the case anyway. But it might have been politically worth fighting – that is we might have thus secured a favourable compromise – if we had enjoyed the united backing of the Parliamentary Party. Unfortunately, there was a hard core of Euro-enthusiasts on the Tory back-benches who instinctively supported the Community in any dispute with Britain. Though a clear minority, they robbed us of the advantages of unity. So, as on previous occasions, I decided not to go down the path of withholding contributions. And we had other cards to play....

The two crucial players would be France – which still held the Presidency [of the European Council] – and Germany. Before the European Assembly election campaign got under way I tried to persuade President Mitterrand and Chancellor Kohl to agree to sort out the budget. In this I was certainly being a 'better' European than they were: for public opinion in Britain was all for intransigence. But I suspect that the French President, at least, was not minded to reach a deal until the elections had come and gone. My attempts failed.

As the [Fontainebleau] Council approached it still seemed to us that President Mitterrand had not yet fully decided between two possible courses of action – a solution which would be a diplomatic triumph for France (in the chair) or a failure which would all be down to 'Perfidious Albion'. Whatever his private political calculations, the French President was now publicly calling for yet another 'relaunch' of the Community, something which was music to Chancellor Kohl's ears. So when we prepared our own paper on the Community's future for the forthcoming summit, I accepted that it should be liberally sprinkled with *communautaire* phrases.

Margaret Thatcher, *The Downing Street Years*, London, 1993, pp. 539–40.

6.11 'Europe – the Future'

Thatcher did, indeed, seem to have begun to learn how to play the Community game of give and take. The British paper presented at Fontainebleau, 'Europe – the Future', could be taken to be pro-European in its praise for the achievements of the Community and in its call for closer co-operation over external affairs and environmental matters. It also held a core message which coincided with her own philosophy.

STRENGTHENING THE COMMUNITY

If the problems of growth, outdated industrial structures and unemployment which affect us all are to be tackled effectively, we must create the genuine common market in goods and services which is envisaged in the Treaty of Rome and will be crucial to our ability to meet the US and Japanese technological challenge. Only by sustained effort to remove remaining obstacles to intra-Community trade can we enable the citizens of Europe to benefit from the dynamic effects of a fully integrated common market with immense purchasing power. The success of the United States in job creation shows what can be achieved when internal barriers to business and trade come down. We must create the conditions in which European businessmen too can build on their strengths and create prosperity and jobs. This means action to harmonize standards and prevent their deliberate use as barriers to intra-Community trade; more rapid and better coordinated customs procedures; a major effort to improve mutual recognition of professional qualifications; and liberalizing trade in services, including banking, insurance and transportation of goods and people.

'Europe – the Future', extracted from the *Journal of Common Market Studies*, Vol. XXIII, No. 1, September 1984, pp. 73–81.

6.12 The 'relaunch' of the European idea

Thatcher was unlucky in that her period as Prime Minister coincided with an upsurge in the 'European idea', which threatened to take the Community far further than she was prepared to go. In 1981 the foreign ministers of Germany and Italy, Hans-Dietrich Genscher and Emilio Colombo, presented a paper to the European Parliament urging further initiatives towards political union. It was an early sign of a renewed thrust towards European integration which was to accelerate over the following ten years. This was not a problem which her five predecessors had had to face.

Revitalizing European Union – Draft European Act

Presenting the drafts Mr. Genscher had this to say:

'... The economic problems now confronting us go to the economic roots of our democracies and of the European Community. Nevertheless, we cannot focus our efforts solely on the economic issues. We must, instead, set our sights on the grand design of the political unification of Europe, for it is from that design that we shall draw the strength to act as one and take decisions, on economic matters and others, which will not simply paper over the cracks but provide forward-looking solutions....'

In his address Mr. Colombo laid particular emphasis on the indissoluble link to be forged between the 'political' and the 'economic', which must converge into a specific European strategy. Among other things, the Italian Foreign Minister said:

'... We are proposing to give renewed impetus to European integration, strengthen the institutions, improve the decision-making process and promote and develop the pragmatic process of political cooperation between our ten countries with the aim of broadening political cooperation to take in security, culture and law enforcement in order to move towards the basic objective of European Union by following a comprehensive approach in which the political, social and economic elements will comple-ment each other.'

Report of the presentation of the Genscher–Colombo plan to the European Parliament, 19 November 1981, from the *Bulletin of the European Communities*, Vol. 11, London, 1981, points 1.2.2 and 1.2.3.

6.13   The Single Market

At Fontainebleau and afterwards, Thatcher's strategy was to appear 'ostentatiously *communautaire*'[21] in her language towards the EC states. Indications during the budgetary dispute that the French and Germans might favour a 'two-tier' Europe, with Britain on the bottom rung, was not compatible with her view of Britain's place in the world. She also genuinely sought the deregularisation of the Community, which neatly complemented her domestic philosophy. Both considerations lay behind the paper 'Europe – the Future' and the development towards the Single European Act (SEA) which it proposed. This way forward was agreed at the Luxembourg European Council in December 1985 and envisioned a Single Market by the end of 1992. Thatcher's mistake lay in believing that she could, in the climate of a European 'relaunch', obtain the Single Market without any serious threat to the powers of Westminster.

I had one overriding positive goal. This was to create a single Common Market. The Community's internal tariffs on goods had been abolished in July 1968. At the same time it had become a customs union, which Britain had fully accepted in July 1977. What remained were the so-called 'non-tariff' barriers. These came in a variety of more or less subtle forms. Different national standards on matters ranging from safety to health, regulations discriminating against foreign products, public procurement policies, delays and overelaborate procedures at customs posts – all these and many others served to frustrate the existence of a real Common Market. British businesses would be among those most likely to benefit from an opening-up of other countries' markets. For example, we were more or less effectively excluded from the important German insurance and financial services markets where I knew – as I suspect did the Germans – that our people would excel. Transport was another important area where we were stopped from making the inroads we wanted. The price we would have to pay to achieve a Single Market with all its economic benefits, though, was more majority voting in the Community. There was no escape from that, because otherwise

[21] Thatcher, *Downing Street Years*, p. 548.

particular countries would succumb to domestic pressures and prevent the opening up of their markets. It also required more power for the European Commission: but that power must be used in order to create and maintain a Single Market rather than to advance other objectives.

I knew that I would have to fight a strong rear-guard action against attempts to weaken Britain's own control over areas of vital national interest to us. I was not going to have majority voting applying, for example, to taxation which the Commission would have liked us to 'harmonise'.... I was not prepared to give up our powers to control immigration (from non-EC countries), to combat terrorism, crime and drug trafficking and to take measures on human, animal and plant health, keeping out carriers of dangerous diseases – all of which required proper frontier controls.... Again, this was an essential matter of national sovereignty, for which a government must answer to its own Parliament and people. I was prepared to go along with some modest increase in the powers of the European Assembly, which would shortly and somewhat inaccurately be described as a Parliament: but the Council of Ministers, representing governments answerable to national Parliaments, must always have the final say. Finally, I was going to resist any attempt to make treaty changes which would allow the Commission – and by majority vote the Council – to pile extra burdens on British businesses.

Thatcher, *Downing Street Years*, pp. 553–4.

6.14   The 'slippery slope towards EMU'

In fact, Thatcher was forced to make more significant concessions than she had envisaged. She had resisted the idea that the SEA be prepared at an inter-government conference (IGC). This implied that there would have to be alterations to the Treaty of Rome and possible institutional changes to the Community, which Thatcher rejected. On this she was outvoted at the Milan Council in the summer of 1985. Though the structural changes which emerged from the IGC in September were modest, she was, significantly, unable to prevent them. Worse was to come. EMU had also found its way into the Single Act, albeit in a muted form. At the December Council meeting in Luxembourg, to the apparent dismay of her Chancellor of the Exchequer, this was accepted by the Prime Minister. The implications, as Lawson pointed out to her, were considerable.

Since I was not to be present at the Luxembourg Council, and the Foreign Office would inevitably be soft on the issue, I minuted Margaret again on Thursday, 28 November 1985, just ahead of the Council which was due to start on the following Monday:

Your line might be:

'There should be no reference in the Treaty to EMU, since this – which implies progress towards a common currency and a common Central Bank – would be no more credible to outside opinion than the commitments entered into in 1971 and 1972, and is in any case politically unacceptable to the UK.'

In the event, she was able, with German support, to get the Treaty reference to EMU watered down, but not removed altogether; and, preferring the on-the-spot advice of the Foreign Office, who told her that what remained was little more than hot air, to the counsel I had proffered in advance, she signed up. The great prize was allegedly the target of completing the single market by the end of 1992 and the facilitation of this by a large scale move from unanimity to majority voting. I was sceptical about the wisdom of the deal she had struck. I felt that we had embarked upon a dangerous slippery slope towards EMU; whereas the move to majority voting, which had been strongly urged by [Jacques] Delors[22] as essential if Europe was to regain the momentum it had latterly lost, would have been agreed even without EMU.

Lawson, *The View From Number 11*, pp. 893–4.

6.15 The Bruges Speech

Once Thatcher had, as Lawson put it, 'sold the pass over EMU'[23] at Luxembourg, it was likely to present her with difficulties from those in the Community who wanted deeper integration. Indeed, having promoted the SEA, it

[22] French Socialist and President of the European Commission, 1984–94.
[23] Lawson, *The View From Number 11*, p. 903.

became increasingly illogical to resist strengthening the powers of those EC institutions which would be necessary to implement it. The task which she now set herself was to prevent Britain being sucked into monetary union, and thence into a United States of Europe. EMU came to the fore at the Hanover European Council in June 1988, when a committee under Jacques Delors, whom Thatcher despised as an arch-federalist, was set up to report on practical steps towards monetary union within the Community. Delors further angered Thatcher by publicly asserting that, ten years on, 80 per cent of Community economic, financial and social legislation was likely to be directed from Brussels, and by an address to the British Trades Union Congress which highlighted the social implications of the SEA. Her riposte came in a speech to the College of Europe in Bruges, on 20 September.

It is ironic that just when those countries, such as the Soviet Union, which have tried to run everything from the centre, are learning that success depends on dispersing power and decisions away from the centre, some in the Community seem to want to move in the opposite direction. We have not successfully rolled back the frontiers of the state in Britain, only to see them reimposed at a European level, with a European super-state exercising a new dominance from Brussels....

Willing and active co-operation between independent sovereign states is the best way to build a successful European Community.... Europe will be stronger precisely because it has France as France, Spain as Spain, Britain as Britain, each with its own customs, traditions and identity. It would be folly to try to fit them into some sort of identikit European personality....

Let Europe be a family of nations, understanding each other better, appreciating each other more, doing more together, but relishing our national identity no less than our common European endeavour. Let us have a Europe which plays its full part in a wider world, which looks outward not inward, and which preserves that Atlantic Community – that Europe on both sides of the Atlantic – which is our noblest inheritance and our greatest strength.

From Thatcher, *Downing Street Years*, pp. 744–5.

6.16 'The ultimate battle'

It may be that the Bruges Speech hardened opposition among the leaders of the EC states against Thatcher. Certainly from then onwards she was unable to avoid the impression that her own version of a deregulated, free-enterprise Europe was under siege. At the Madrid Council in the summer of 1989, she felt the need to abandon the formula on Britain's membership of the ERM which she had held to since 1979 – that Britain would join 'when the time was right' – to state more specific conditions of entry. This fitted with the first stage of the Delors Report on progress towards EMU. In October 1990 Thatcher, reluctantly, accepted that Britain should join the ERM. At the Rome summit in the same month, however, she assertively, but unsuccessfully, resisted a decision to implement the next phase of the Delors Report – the transitional stage towards a European central bank – and a Franco-German proposal for a second IGC on political unification to run parallel with one already looking into monetary union.

The atmosphere [at Rome] went from bad to worse. The others were determined to insert in the communiqué provisions on political union, none of which I was prepared to accept. I said that I would not pre-empt the debate in the IGC and had a unilateral observation to this effect incorporated in the text. They also insisted on following the German proposal that Stage 2 of monetary union should begin on 1 January 1994. I would not accept this either. I had inserted in the communiqué the sentence:

> The United Kingdom, while ready to move beyond Stage 1 through the creation of a new monetary institution and a common Community currency, believes that decisions on the substance of that move should precede decisions on its timing.

They were not interested in compromise. My objections were heard in stony silence. I now had no support. I just had to say no.

In three years the European Community had gone from practical decisions about restoring order to the Community's finances to grandiose schemes of monetary and political union with firm timetables but no agreed substance – all without open, principled public debate on these questions either nationally or in

European fora. Now at Rome the ultimate battle for the future of the Community had been joined. But I would have to return to London to win another battle on which the outcome in Europe would depend – that for the soul of the Parliamentary Conservative Party.

Thatcher, *Downing Street Years*, p. 767.

6.17 Nemesis

By this time, many in her government who were by no means 'Euro-fanatics' were deeply dismayed by her continuous conflict with the EC. Her change of position on the ERM at the Madrid meeting came about, in part at least, because she was, to use her own word, 'ambushed' by Geoffrey Howe, her Foreign Secretary, and the Chancellor, Nigel Lawson. Lawson was to resign in October 1989 on issues related to ERM entry. Howe followed a year later, perturbed by Thatcher's intemperate outbursts at the Rome Council. Even her like-minded friends proved unhelpful. The Trade and Industry Secretary, Nicholas Ridley, left Thatcher further exposed when he felt obliged to resign after indiscreetly castigating monetary union as 'a German racket' in an interview to a political journal. Europe was not Thatcher's only problem. An ailing economy and severe public opposition to the 'poll tax' both contributed to the Prime Minister increasingly being viewed by her party as an electoral liability. The importance of the European issue was, however, highlighted by Howe in his resignation speech in the Commons, which was to precipitate the party leadership challenge, which Thatcher lost.

Sir Geoffrey Howe (Surrey East) ... It was a great honour to serve for six years as Foreign and Commonwealth Secretary and to share with my Right Hon. Friend in some notable achievements in the European Community – from Fontainebleau to the Single European Act. But it was as we moved on to consider the crucial monetary issues in the European context that I came to feel increasing concern. Some of the reasons for that anxiety were made clear by my Right Hon. Friend the Member for Blaby (Mr. Lawson) in his resignation speech just over 2 months ago. Like him, I concluded at least five years ago that the conduct of our policy against inflation could no longer rest solely on attempts to measure and control the domestic money supply. We had no doubt that we would be helped in that battle, and, indeed, in other respects, by joining the exchange rate mechanism of the European monetary system....

It is now, alas, impossible to resist the conclusion that today's higher rates of inflation could well have been avoided had the question of ERM membership been properly considered and resolved at a much earlier stage. There are I fear developing grounds for similar anxiety over the handling – not just at and after the Rome summit – of the wider, much more open question of economic and monetary union....

It was the late Lord Stockton, formerly Harold Macmillan, who put the central point clearly. As long ago as 1962, he argued that we had to place and keep ourselves within the EC. He saw it as essential then, as it is today, not to cut ourselves off from the realities of power; not to retreat into a ghetto of sentimentality about our past and so diminish our own control over our own destiny in the future

The pity is that the Macmillan view had not been perceived more clearly a decade before in the 1950s. It would have spared us so many of the struggles of the last 20 years had we been in the Community from the outset; had we been ready, in the much too simple phrase, to 'surrender some sovereignty' at a much earlier stage.

If we had been in from the start, as almost everybody now acknowledges, we should have had more, not less, influence over the Europe in which we live today. We should never forget the lesson of that isolation, of being on the outside looking in, for the conduct of today's affairs.... We must at all costs avoid presenting ourselves yet again with an oversimplified choice, a false antithesis, a bogus dilemma, between one alternative, starkly labelled 'cooperation between independent sovereign states' and a second, equally crudely labelled alternative, 'centralised federal super-state', as if there were no middle way in between.

We commit a serious error if we think always in terms of 'surrendering' sovereignty and seek to stand pat for all time on a given deal by proclaiming, as my Right Hon. Friend the Prime Minister did two weeks ago that we have 'surrendered enough'....

There is talk of course of a single currency for Europe. I agree that there are many difficulties about the concept – both economic and political. Of course, as I said in my letter of resignation, none of us wants the imposition of a single currency. But that is not the real risk. The 11 others cannot impose their solution on the 12th country against its will, but they can go ahead without us. The risk is not imposition but isolation. The real threat is leaving ourselves with no say in the monetary arrangements that the rest of Europe chose for itself with Britain, once again, scrambling to join the club later, when the rules have been set and after power has been distributed by others to our disadvantage. That would be the worst possible outcome....

The point was perhaps more sharply put by a British business-man, trading in Brussels and elsewhere, who wrote to me last week, stating:

> 'People throughout Europe see our Prime Minister's finger-wagging and her passionate "No, No, No", much more clearly than the carefully worded texts'.

He went on:

> 'It is too easy for them to believe that we all share her attitudes; for why else has she been our Prime Minister for so long?'

My correspondent concluded:

> 'This is a desperately serious situation for our country.'

And sadly, I have to agree.

United Kingdom Parliamentary Debates, House of Commons, 6th Series, Volume 180, London, 1990, 13 November 1990, cols 461–5.

6.18 The saloon-bar xenophobe

Margaret Thatcher had her own vision for Europe, to restructure it in the way she had reshaped Britain – to 'Thatcherise' it. There are those who accept this as both a realisable and a respectable position. Whether there is 'no alternative' to deeper and wider integration in Europe remains, as yet, debatable. Her view, however, stemmed from a set of narrow, nationalistic perceptions which made her innately distrustful 'of that un-British combination of high-flown rhetoric and pork-barrel politics which passed for European statesmanship'.[24] She shared, in a heightened form perhaps, the perception of many of her generation that Europeans were difficult, unreliable, prone to gushes of 'Euro-idealism' and needed saving from themselves. There was also the lingering belief that Britain's real interests were Atlanticist.

For Margaret, the special relationship with the United States was all-important, and she regarded the continental Europeans with distrust and, in private, with undisguised distaste and hostility. Germany, in particular, increasingly became the butt of the visceral sentiments she had developed during the war. I have no doubt that the reason why Nick Ridley felt it was safe to make the anti-German remarks in his *Spectator* interview which were to lead to his enforced and reluctant resignation in 1990, was that he had many times heard Margaret utter precisely the same sentiments in private – as, indeed, had I. Margaret was, of course, at all times a politician; and I was never entirely sure how much the saloon-bar xenophobia of her later years represented her own uninhibited feelings and how far she saw it as a potential vote winner. Both elements were present.

Lawson, *The View From Number 11*, p. 900.

6.19 Maastricht and after

The new Prime Minister, John Major, presided over important developments in Europe. The Single Market came into being in January 1993. In the same year, partly in the wake of the SEA and also because of the convulsions in Eastern Europe, which produced pressure to increase the size of the EC, the Community embraced members of EFTA in an association called the European Economic Area. Before this, however, in December 1991, the two IGCs on political and monetary union reported to the European Council at Maastricht in December 1991 and produced agreement to conclude a new treaty to provide for deeper and wider union in Europe – developing the EC into the

---

[24] Thatcher, *Downing Street Years*, p. 727.

EU. Though certainly no federalist, Major was eager to assert Britain's European credentials after the Thatcher experience. On the other hand, he had inherited a deeply divided party, especially on Europe, and a principal objective, like Wilson's before him, was not to widen this fissure. The result was a treaty which, though it pushed European union a step further, was also a compromise which permitted Britain to opt out of two central clauses, on monetary union and Community social policy.

The significant concessions which Major won at Maastricht failed to appease increasingly vociferous anti-Europeans in the Conservative Party who, fired by Britain's ignominious forced withdrawal from the ERM on 'Black Wednesday', 16 September 1992, were to harass the ratification of the treaty as it proceeded through the Commons. In November 1994 nine Conservative MPs were deprived of the party whip after voting against the Bill to increase contributions to the EU (though they returned to the fold in the spring of 1995). This was just the tip of the iceberg, and 'Euro-phobes' existed at Cabinet level too. There were serious doubts whether the Party could avoid a permanent split over Europe. In these circumstances, Major fell back upon a formula of 'variable geometry', as he called it at the Leiden European Council of 1994, to describe the way forward for the Community. Meanwhile, he was committed to another IGC in 1996, which would review the operation of the Maastricht Treaty and probably seek to increase the institutional powers of the EU. In late 1994, during a rare moment when things seemed generally to be going right for the government, the pro-Europe *Guardian* had this to say.

Europe will not be on the agenda at the Bournemouth [Party] Conference, and will be touted on the fringe only by a mis-begotten alliance between Sir James Goldsmith,[25] a protectionist who now chooses to speak for Britain from a leadership position among the French near-fascist right, and Lord Tebbit,[26] who when last in office was believed to be a free trader. Even in the face of more menacing critics, whether sceptic or integrationist,

---

[25] Millionaire financier and Euro-MP.
[26] Cabinet minister under Thatcher and a 'Euro-sceptic'.

Major feels he is starting to get his language right. The multi-speed, multi-layer European Union for which he spoke at Leiden is a proposition he thinks will release him from most of his problems, especially if he can find a language with which to say what he really means: that different parts of Europe necessarily have different *agendas*.

Adding to his confidence, allegedly, was his refusal to give promotion to any minister who had stepped an inch out of line. The [Michael] Portillo[27] move to Employment was treated in this context, as a demotion. Michael Howard,[28] having spent two years courting every far-right pressure group, is confidently seen as a man in his last job.

All this, however, is a touch fanciful. Europe has not gone away. One great parliamentary battle remains to be decided, when the bill comes forward, as it must soon, to increase the national subvention to the European Union. The sceptics can hardly let it pass: the Ulster Unionists[29] will have to be summoned again. But there remains the deeper battle over what sort of party, on this matter, the Conservatives any longer are. When the manifesto comes to be written, before, during or after the 1996 intergovernmental conference of the EU, how Portilloite will Major decide it is prudent to be? The lineage will be termed, respectably, Gaullist.

Gaullism is becoming a fashionable label even in pro-European ministerial circles. The General, one is reminded, was a true European. But for Major, the positioning on Europe is undecided. It's a question that will put under greatest strain his new seduction by the call of historic destiny. Shall he opt for the larger British future, or the smaller but more pressing fate of the Conservative Party?

The Guardian, 11 October 1994.

---

[27] A leading 'anti-European' minister.

[28] Home Secretary in Major's government.

[29] Major needed the votes of the Ulster Unionist MPs to obtain ratification of the Maastricht Treaty in the summer of 1993.

Guide to further reading

General

The best background to the European context is provided by Derek W. Urwin, *The Community of Europe: A History of European Integration Since 1945*, London, 1995. More detail and a more polemical approach is offered by Alan S. Milward in *The Reconstruction of Western Europe 1945–51*, London, 1984, and *The European Rescue of the Nation State*, London, 1994. Valuable essays on the early stages of European integration are to be found in two volumes edited by Ennio Di Nolfo: *Power in Europe? I: Great Britain, France, Italy and Germany in a Post-War World, 1945–50*, Berlin and New York, 1984, and *Power in Europe? II: Great Britain, France, Germany and Italy and the Origins of the EEC, 1952–57*, Berlin and New York, 1992. A survey of Britain's response to integration is provided by Sean Greenwood, *Britain and European Co-operation Since 1945*, Oxford, 1992, and in John W. Young, *Britain and European Unity, 1945–1992*, London, 1993. Brian Brivati and Harriet Jones (eds), *From Reconstruction to Integration: Britain and Europe Since 1945*, Leicester, 1993, provide a useful collection of essays. Primary sources may be found in the three volumes of W. Lipgens and W. Loth (eds), *Documents on the History of European Integration*, Berlin, 1985–88, and oral evidence from significant participants, especially on the British side, is produced in Michael Charlton, *The Price of Victory*, London, 1983.

The Labour governments and European integration 1945–51

Aspects of Ernest Bevin's European policy are to be found in: John W. Young, *Britain, France and the Unity of Europe 1945–51*, Leicester, 1984; John Kent, 'The British Empire and the origins of the Cold War', in Anne Deighton (ed.), *Britain and the*

First Cold War, London, 1990; Sean Greenwood, 'Ernest Bevin, France and "Western Union": August 1945 – February 1946', *European History Quarterly*, Vol. 14, 1984; and Sean Greenwood, 'The Third Force in the late 1940s', in Brivati and Jones (eds), *From Reconstruction to Integration*. A pioneering work which remains helpful is R. B. Manderson-Jones, *The Special Relationship: Anglo-American Relations and Western European Unity 1947–56*, London, 1972. Bevin and the Atlantic Alliance are covered effectively in John Baylis, *The Diplomacy of Pragmatism: Britain and the Formation of NATO, 1942–49*, London, 1993. Primary documentation is published in Roger Bullen and M. E. Pelly, *Documents on British Policy Overseas, Series II, Volume I: The Schuman Plan, The Council of Europe and Western European Integration 1950–52*, London, 1986.

Britain and the European Defence Community

The most detailed account of this is Saki Dockrill's, *Britain's Policy for West German Rearmament, 1950–5*, Cambridge, 1991. A more condensed interpretation is provided by David Weigall in 'British perceptions of the European Defence Community', in Peter M. R. Stirk and David Willis (eds), *Shaping Postwar Europe: European Unity and Disunity 1945–57*, London, 1991. Two indispensable essays by John W. Young on Churchill and Eden's attitudes towards Europe are, 'Churchill's "No" to Europe: the "rejection" of European union by Churchill's post-war government, 1951–52', *Historical Journal*, Vol. 28, 1985, and 'The Schuman Plan and British association' in John W. Young (ed.), *The Foreign Policy of Churchill's Peacetime Administration, 1951–55*, Leicester, 1988. Some of the related documents are published in Roger Bullen and M. E. Pelly (eds), *Documents on British Policy Overseas, Series II, Volume III: German Rearmament, September–December 1950*, London, 1989.

From Messina to Britain's first application 1955–61

There is still little detailed work on this period and the standard analysis remains Miriam Camps' admirable *Britain and the*

European Community, 1955–63, Oxford, 1964. The prolific John W. Young has contributed an important assessment in '"The parting of the ways?" Britain, the Messina Conference and the Spaak Committee, June–December 1955', in Michael Dockrill and John W. Young (eds), *British Foreign Policy 1945–56*, London, 1989. Wolfram Kaiser has written a stimulating essay on possible motives behind Macmillan's decision in 1961, 'To join or not to join? The "appeasement" policy of Britain's first EEC application', in Brivati and Jones, *From Reconstruction to Integration*. The second volume of Alistair Horne's official biography, *Macmillan 1957–1986*, London, 1989, is useful on Europe, but less so than John Turner's, *Macmillan*, London, 1994. Three volumes of Macmillan's autobiography which cover this period have relevant primary material, including extracts from his diaries. These are: *Riding the Storm 1956–59*, London, 1971; *Pointing the Way 1959–61*, London, 1972; and *At the End of the Day 1961–63*, London, 1973. *The Robert Hall Diaries 1954–61*, London, 1991, edited by Alec Cairncross, and Robert Marjolin's *Architect of European Unity: Memoirs 1911–1986*, London, 1989, give insights into the official mind on both sides of the Channel.

Into the Community 1961–73

This is where memoirs and published private diaries come into their own, in allowing some, quite detailed, construction of events to be made. The period is particularly rich in the accounts of Labour participants. The first volume of Harold Wilson's memoirs, *The Labour Government, 1964–70*, London, 1971, is rather bland, especially when read alongside the more lively, sometimes self-serving, diaries of his political colleagues. The best of these for this period are Barbara Castle, *The Castle Diaries, 1964–70*, London, 1984, and the first two volumes of the ministerial diaries of Richard Crossman, *Diaries of a Cabinet Minister, Volume I: Minister of Housing, 1964–66*, London, 1975, and *Volume II: Lord President of the Council and Leader of the House of Commons, 1966–68*, London, 1976. George Brown's autobiography, *In My Way*, Harmondsworth, 1972, is typically revealing. More prosaic, but helpful, documentation is collected in Uwe Kitzinger, *The European Common Market and the Community*, London, 1967. Material on the Heath government remains sparse. The fullest treatment of Heath's European objectives in the years 1970–74 is in John W. Young, *The Heath Government and British Entry into the European Community*, Leicester, 1995.

Britain in Europe 1973–94

Again, there is a good selection of diaries and memoirs available. Alongside Barbara Castle, *The Castle Diaries, 1974–76*, London, 1980, there are the volumes of Tony Benn's diaries, with *Against the Tide, Diaries 1973–76*, London, 1990, being the most revealing on European issues. The pro-European voice, often from the heart of the Community, is given by Roy Jenkins in his autobiography, *A Life at the Centre*, London, 1992, and in his diaries as President of the European Commission, *European Diary 1977–81*, London, 1989. Nicholas Henderson, ambassador to Bonn and Paris in the early years of British membership, gives a critical view of the Labour government in *Mandarin: The Diaries of an Ambassador 1969–1982*, London, 1994. The *alumni* of the Thatcher governments have not been reticent to explain themselves in memoir form. Most have little of interest to say on Europe. Indispensable, however, are those of the Prime Minister, Margaret Thatcher, *The Downing Street Years*, London, 1993, and those of her long-serving Chancellor of the Exchequer, Nigel Lawson, *The View from Number 11: Memoirs of a Tory Radical*, London, 1993. Anthony King's *Britain Says Yes: The 1975 Referendum on the Common Market*, Washington, 1977, is the most lively assessment of this subject. The only detailed overview of this period is Stephen George's informative *An Awkward Partner: Britain in the European Community*, Oxford, 1990.

Index

The acronyms used most frequently in the text are given here in bold.